The Globe Reader's Collection

STORIES
TO LIVE BY

GLOBE FEARON
Pearson Learning Group

Project Reviewers:
Laurie J. Tyson, English Teacher
Minneapolis Public Schools
Minneapolis, Minnesota

Kim Erwin, Eighth Grade English Teacher,
   School Theatre Director
Clay-Chalk Middle School
Trussville, Alabama

Senior Editor: Lynn Kloss

Project Editor: Wendy R. Diskin

Development House: Publishers Resource Group, Inc.

Production Editor: Travis Bailey

Marketing Manager: Lisa Sandick

Electronic Page Production: José Lopez, Leslie Greenberg

Cover and Interior Design: Sharon Ferguson

Cover Art: Marc Chagall's *The Feast of Purim,* Copyright ARS, NY

Illustrator: Mike Biegle

ISBN 0-835-94847-1
Printed in the United States of America

3 4 5 6 7 8 9 10 11 12 05 04 03 02

1-800-321-3106
www.pearsonlearning.com

TABLE OF CONTENTS

UNIT 3: A COMMON PURPOSE

READING STORIES TO LIVE BY

The stories in this book, both fiction and nonfiction, come from cultures all over the world. They reveal universal human traits, such as courage, loyalty, fairness, generosity, and compassion. Identifying with a character in a story can give insight into your own character, showing that through literature we can learn not only about shared human experiences, but also about ourselves as individuals.

The selections in this book include:

Legends. A legend is a story that has been told over and over again. As legends are repeated, the details become more and more elaborate and the characters more and more extraordinary. Often, an element of the supernatural or magical is present, as in the legend, "The Magic Boat."

Folktales. A folktale is a story that was also first told aloud for many years before it was written. "The Dancing Kettle" is a retelling of a popular folk tale that has been passed down through generations in Japan.

Short stories. "The Gentleman of Río en Medio" is an example of a short story, or an original story that was invented by the author.

Nonfiction accounts. The nonfiction selections, such as "from *Woodsong*," relate events that happened in real life.

Each selection in this book was chosen because of its value as a quality piece of literature from the culture it represents and because it offers a positive message about character.

THE WORLD WITHIN

The first unit of this book focuses on values and character traits related to *self*. The characters in these selections have experiences that cause them to learn about, test, and strengthen their own values. Each selection highlights a particular character trait. For example, "The Wise Master" teaches a lesson about trusting your own conscience to make the right decisions. In "The No-Guitar Blues," a boy learns the importance of taking responsibility for his own actions. The unit ends with Helen Keller telling her amazing true story of patience and persistence in the selection, "Helen Keller and Anne Sullivan."

REACHING OUT

This unit is made up of selections that emphasize the relationship between *self and others*. New experiences unfold for these characters who learn to make a connection with a fellow human being. In "Damon and Pythias . . . the Perfect Friendship," for example, loyalty between friends is put to the test. In another selection, a boy unexpectedly receives the charity of a woman he was trying to mug in "Thank You, M'am." The autobiographical account "A Mason-Dixon Memory" is the last relationship explored in this unit. In this selection, a man remembers what he learned from loyal friends who stood by his side when he was a child.

A COMMON PURPOSE

The relationship between *self and community* is the focus of the third unit of this book. The characters in this unit know, or come to realize, the importance of acting for the common good of their community. Selections, such as "How War Was Ended," explain how a brave warrior saved his people from continuous battle. In another selection, a man shares his true story about proudly serving his country during WWII in "Navajo Code Talker." For the closing thoughts on this unit, Anne Frank, a young woman growing up during the Holocaust, shares her optimistic hopes for her suffering community in an excerpt from "The Diary of a Young Girl."

CARETAKERS OF THE EARTH

The last unit of this book explores the relationship between *self and nature*. Characters are inspired by man and beast alike in these pages, and they often appreciate aspects of nature that they previously had taken for granted. For example, a hunter discovers how little he really knows about animal relationships in "The Sparrow." Or, there is the story of how children helped save thousands of acres of endangered rain forest in "Founders of the Children's Rain Forest." Unit four closes with a reading from "Cub Life," a true story about a couple who adopt and raise three orphaned lion cubs.

"This above all: to thine own self be true." — William Shakespeare

Unit 1
THE WORLD WITHIN

THE WISE MASTER

retold by Heather Forest

If a person who is considered to be knowledgeable and wise makes a statement, that statement is usually taken to be true. What if such a person advises a group of people to do something that is dishonest or otherwise against their ideals and sense of integrity? Whom should they trust, the "wise" person or themselves?

In this tale from India, students trust a wise teacher. He orders the students to do something that puzzles and concerns them. They must decide whether to do as they are told or to question the orders they are given.

VOCABULARY WORDS

temple (tem′pəl) a building for the worship of a religious figure
❖ The bells for the early morning service in the *temple* ring at dawn.

meditation (med′ə tā′shən) deep, continuous thinking on sacred matters
❖ The priest's *meditation* lasts an hour each morning and evening.

defile (dē fīl′) to corrupt; to make dirty
❖ They do not want to *defile* the beautiful park by littering.

immoral (im môr′əl) unethical; wicked
❖ Such *immoral* acts would shock the good-hearted townspeople.

retorted (ri tôrt′id) replied quickly
❖ "But I don't like broccoli," the child *retorted*.

integrity (in teg′rə tē) sound moral principle
❖ Their *integrity* has earned them everyone's trust.

 **There once was a teacher** who lived with a great number of students in a run-down temple. The students supported themselves by begging for food in the bustling streets of a nearby town. Some of the students grumbled about their humble living conditions. In response, the old master said one day, "We must repair the walls of this temple. Since we occupy ourselves with study and meditation, there is no time to earn the money we will need. I have thought of a simple solution."

All the students eagerly gathered closer to hear the words of their teacher. The master said, "Each of you must go into the town and steal goods that can be sold for money. In this way, we will be able to do the good work of repairing our temple."

The students were startled at this suggestion from their wise master. But since they respected him greatly, they assumed he must have good judgment and did not protest.

The wise master said sternly, "In order not to defile our excellent reputation by committing illegal and immoral acts, please be certain to steal when no one is looking. I do not want anyone to be caught."

When the teacher walked away, the students discussed the plan among themselves. "It is wrong to steal," said one. "Why has our wise master asked us to do this?"

Another retorted, "It will allow us to build our temple, which is a good result."

They all agreed that their teacher was wise and just and must have a sensible reason for making such an unusual request. They set out eagerly for the town, promising each other that they would not disgrace their school by getting caught. "Be careful," they called to one another. "Do not let anyone see you stealing."

All the students except one young boy set forth. The wise master approached him and asked, "Why do you stay behind?"

The boy responded, "I cannot follow your instructions to steal where no one will see me. Wherever I go, I am always there watching. My own eyes will see me steal."

The wise master tearfully embraced the boy. "I was just testing the integrity of my students," he said. "You are the only one who has passed the test!"

The boy went on to become a great teacher himself.

READING FOR UNDERSTANDING

1. Where do the students and their wise master live?

2. How do the students spend their days?

3. What does the master tell the students they must do?

4. How do most of the students react to this order?

5. How does the main character, the boy, react?

RESPONDING TO THE STORY

The master's intent is to test the students' integrity to see if they will stand up for their own beliefs and ideals. Have you ever been faced with a choice between obeying an order or refusing one because it went against your own sense of integrity? If not, then how about anyone you know or may have read about? In a short paragraph, discuss the choice that either you or the other person made.

REVIEWING VOCABULARY

Fill in each blank with the correct word from the following list: *temple, retorted, meditation, defile, immoral.*

1. I didn't want to disturb the priest during his

_____ .

2. People have been worshiping in this
_____ for hundreds of years.

3. I have always believed that lying is _____ .

4. "My client is innocent," the lawyer _____ .

5. Losing the big game would _____ his reputation as a star athlete.

THINKING CRITICALLY

1. The master tests the students' integrity by ordering them to do something wrong for what seems like a good reason. Do you think this is a good way to test a person's integrity? Why or why not?

2. Why does the master test his students' integrity?

WRITING PROJECTS

1. Imagine that you are a student at the temple. Write a journal entry about the events of the day described in the tale and what you learned from them.

2. Write a scene in which the students return to the temple and the master speaks to them about the stolen goods. Keep in mind that the master had secretly hoped that they would not steal the goods.

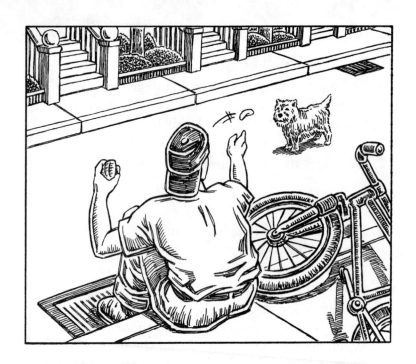

THE NO-GUITAR BLUES
by Gary Soto

*Is it possible to transform a wrong into a right? Living
up to your own personal sense of right and wrong can
sometimes be a challenge. If put to a test, would you be
able to hold yourself accountable for your own actions?*

*Fausto, the main character in this short story by Gary
Soto, loves the music of the group Los Lobos and wants to
learn to play the guitar and start his own band. He has a
serious problem, however: He has no guitar. As you read
the story, look for how Fausto decides to solve his problem.
Then think about the consequences of his decision.*

VOCABULARY WORDS

mission (mish´ən) a calling or purpose in life
❖ My brother believes that his *mission* in life is to become a doctor.

perpetual (pər pech´o͞o əl) continuing indefinitely
❖ The *perpetual* rocking of the boat made me seasick.

empanada (em pə nä´də) a Spanish or Latin American pastry turnover filled with meat, vegetables, or fruit
❖ They like to have pumpkin *empanadas* for dessert.

confession (kən fesh´ən) a formal admittance of sin or wrongdoing, sometimes to a priest
❖ His guilt over hurting his brother led him to make a *confession*.

lector (lek´tər) a person who reads lessons in a church service
❖ At the church service, the *lector* made the announcements in a strong voice.

papas (pä´ päs) Spanish word for potatoes
❖ This restaurant is famous for the way they make *papas*.

chorizo con huevos (chō rē´zō kôn wä´vōs) Spanish for sausage with eggs
❖ *Chorizo con huevos* is a popular breakfast in Mexico.

guitarron (gē tä rōn´) Spanish word for a large guitar
❖ Her uncle plays the *guitarron* in a mariachi band.

hijo (ē´hō) Spanish word for son
❖ My grandmother calls my father "*hijo*."

9

The moment **Fausto saw** the group Los Lobos on "American Bandstand," he knew exactly what he wanted to do with his life—play guitar. His eyes grew large with excitement as Los Lobos ground out a song while teenagers bounced off each other on the crowded dance floor.

He had watched "American Bandstand" for years and had heard Ray Camacho and the Teardrops at Romain Playground, but it had never occurred to him that he too might become a musician. That afternoon Fausto knew his mission in life: to play guitar in his own band; to sweat out his songs and prance around the stage; to make money and dress weird.

Fausto turned off the television set and walked outside, wondering how he could get enough money to buy a guitar. He couldn't ask his parents because they would just say, "Money doesn't grow on trees" or "What do you think we are, bankers?" And besides, they hated rock music. They were into the *conjunto* music of Lydia Mendoza, Flaco Jimenez, and Little Joe and La Familia. And, as Fausto recalled, the last album they bought was *The Chipmunks Sing Christmas Favorites.*

But what the heck, he'd give it a try. He returned inside and watched his mother make tortillas. He leaned against the kitchen counter, trying to work up the nerve to ask her for a guitar. Finally, he couldn't hold back any longer.

"Mom," he said, "I want a guitar for Christmas."

She looked up from rolling tortillas. "Honey, a guitar costs a lot of money."

"How 'bout for my birthday next year," he tried again.

"I can't promise," she said, turning back to her tortillas, "but we'll see."

Fausto walked back outside with a buttered tortilla.

He knew his mother was right. His father was a warehouseman at Berven Rugs, where he made good money but not enough to buy everything his children wanted. Fausto decided to mow lawns to earn money and was pushing the mower down the street before he realized it was winter and no one would hire him. He returned the mower and picked up a rake. He hopped onto his sister's bike (his had two flat tires) and rode north to the nicer section of Fresno in search of work. He went door-to-door, but after three hours he managed to get only one job, and not to rake leaves. He was asked to hurry down to the store to buy a loaf of bread, for which he received a grimy, dirt-caked quarter.

He also got an orange, which he ate sitting at the curb. While he was eating, a dog walked up and sniffed his leg. Fausto pushed him away and threw an orange peel skyward. The dog caught it and ate it in one gulp. The dog looked at Fausto and wagged his tail for more. Fausto tossed him a slice of orange, and the dog snapped it up and licked his lips.

"How come you like oranges, dog?"

The dog blinked a pair of sad eyes and whined.

"What's the matter? Cat got your tongue?" Fausto laughed at his joke and offered the dog another slice.

At that moment a dim light came on inside Fausto's head. He saw that it was sort of a fancy dog, a terrier or something, with dog tags and a shiny collar. And it looked well fed and healthy. In his neighborhood, the dogs were never licensed, and if they got sick they were placed near the water heater until they got well.

This dog looked like he belonged to rich people. Fausto cleaned his juice-sticky hands on his pants and got to his feet. The light in his head grew brighter. It just might work. He called the dog, patted its muscular back, and bent down to check the license.

"Great," he said. "There's an address."

The dog's name was Roger, which struck Fausto as weird because he'd never heard of a dog with a human name. Dogs should have names like Bomber, Freckles, Queenie, Killer, and Zero.

Fausto planned to take the dog home and collect a reward. He would say he had found Roger near the freeway. That would scare the daylights out of the owners, who would be so happy that they would probably give him a reward. He felt bad about lying, but the dog was loose. And it might even really be lost because the address was six blocks away.

Fausto stashed the rake and his sister's bike behind a bush and, tossing an orange peel every time Roger became distracted, walked the dog to his house. He hesitated on the porch until Roger began to scratch the door with a muddy paw. Fausto had come this far, so he figured he might as well go through with it. He knocked softly. When no one answered, he rang the doorbell. A man in a silky bathrobe and slippers opened the door and seemed confused by the sight of his dog and the boy.

"Sir," Fausto said, gripping Roger by the collar. "I found your dog by the freeway. His dog license says he lives here." Fausto looked down at the dog, then up to the man. "He does, doesn't he?"

The man stared at Fausto a long time before saying in a pleasant voice, "That's right." He pulled his robe tighter around him because of the cold and asked Fausto to come in. "So he was by the freeway?"

"Uh-huh."

"You bad, snoopy dog," said the man, wagging his finger. "You probably knocked over some trash cans, too, didn't you?"

Fausto didn't say anything. He looked around, amazed by this house with its shiny furniture and a television as large as the front window at home. Warm bread smells filled the air and music full of soft tinkling floated in from another room.

"Helen," the man called to the kitchen. "We have a visitor." His wife came into the living room wiping her hands on a dish towel and smiling. "And who have we here?" she asked in one of the softest voices Fausto had ever heard.

"This young man said he found Roger near the freeway."

Fausto repeated his story to her while staring at a perpetual clock with a bell-shaped glass, the kind his aunt got when she celebrated her twenty-fifth anniversary. The lady frowned and said, wagging a finger at Roger, "Oh, you're a bad boy."

"It was very nice of you to bring Roger home," the man said. "Where do you live?"

"By that vacant lot on Olive," he said. "You know, by Brownie's Flower Place."

The wife looked at her husband, then Fausto. Her eyes twinkled triangles of light as she said, "Well, young man, you're probably hungry. How about a turnover?"

"What do I have to turn over?" Fausto asked, thinking she was talking about yard work or something like turning trays of dried raisins.

"No, no, dear, it's a pastry." She took him by the elbow and guided him to a kitchen that sparkled with copper pans and bright yellow wallpaper. She guided him to the kitchen table and gave him a tall glass of milk and something that looked like an *empanada*. Steamy waves of heat escaped when he tore it in two. He ate with both eyes on the man and woman who stood arm in arm smiling at him. They were strange, he thought. But nice.

"That was good," he said after he finished the turnover. "Did you make it, ma'am?"

"Yes, I did. Would you like another?"

"No, thank you. I have to go home now."

As Fausto walked to the door, the man opened his wallet and took out a bill. "This is for you," he said. "Roger is special to us, almost like a son."

Fausto looked at the bill and knew he was in trouble. Not with these nice folks or with his parents but with himself. How could he have been so deceitful? The dog wasn't lost. It was just having a fun Saturday walking around.

"I can't take that."

"You have to. You deserve it, believe me," the man said.

"No, I don't."

"Now don't be silly," said the lady. She took the bill from her husband and stuffed it into Fausto's shirt pocket. "You're a lovely child. Your parents are lucky to have you. Be good. And come see us again, please."

Fausto went out, and the lady closed the door. Fausto clutched the bill through his shirt pocket. He felt like ringing the doorbell and begging them to please take the money back, but he knew they would refuse. He hurried away, and at the end of the block, pulled the bill from his shirt pocket: it was a crisp twenty-dollar bill.

"Oh, man, I shouldn't have lied," he said under his breath as he started up the street like a zombie. He wanted to run to church for Saturday confession, but it was past four-thirty, when confession stopped.

He returned to the bush where he had hidden the rake and his sister's bike and rode home slowly, not daring to touch the money in his pocket. At home, in the privacy of his room, he examined the twenty-dollar bill. He had never had so much money. It was probably enough to buy a secondhand guitar. But he felt bad, like the time he stole a dollar from the secret fold inside his older brother's wallet.

Fausto went outside and sat on the fence. "Yeah," he said. "I can probably get a guitar for twenty. Maybe at a yard sale—things are cheaper."

His mother called him to dinner.

The next day he dressed for church without anyone telling him. He was going to go to eight o'clock mass.

"I'm going to church, Mom," he said. His mother was in the kitchen cooking *papas* and *chorizo con huevos*. A pile of tortillas lay warm under a dishtowel.

"Oh, I'm so proud of you, my son." She beamed, turning over the crackling *papas*.

His older brother, Lawrence, who was at the table reading the funnies, mimicked, "Oh, I'm so proud of you, my son," under his breath.

At Saint Theresa's he sat near the front. When Father Jerry began by saying that we are all sinners, Fausto thought he looked straight at him. Could he know? Fausto fidgeted with guilt. No, he thought. I only did it yesterday.

Fausto knelt, prayed, and sang. But he couldn't forget the man and the lady, whose names he didn't even know, and the *empanada* they had given him. It had a strange name but tasted really good. He wondered how they got rich. And how that dome clock worked. He had asked his mother once how his aunt's clock worked. She said it just worked, the way the refrigerator works. It just did.

Fausto caught his mind wandering and tried to concentrate on his sins. He said a Hail Mary and sang, and when the wicker basket came his way, he stuck a hand reluctantly in his pocket and pulled out the twenty-dollar bill. He ironed it between his palms and dropped it into the basket. The grownups stared. Here was a kid dropping twenty dollars in the basket while they gave just three or four dollars.

There would be a second collection for Saint Vincent de Paul, the lector announced. The wicker baskets again floated in the pews, and this time the adults around him, given a second chance to show their charity, dug deep into their wallets and purses and dropped in fives and tens. This time Fausto tossed in the grimy quarter.

Fausto felt better after church. He went home and played football in the front yard with his brother and some neighbor kids. He felt cleared of wrongdoing and was so happy that he played one of his best games of football ever. On one play, he tore his good pants, which he knew he shouldn't have been wearing. For a second, while he examined the hole, he wished he hadn't given the twenty dollars away.

Man, I coulda bought me some Levis, he thought. He pictured his twenty dollars being spent to buy church candles. He pictured a priest buying an armful of flowers with *his* money.

Fausto had to forget about getting a guitar. He spent the next day playing soccer in his good pants, which were now his old pants. But that night during dinner, his mother said she remembered seeing an old bass *guitarron* the last time she cleaned out her father's garage.

"It's a little dusty," his mom said, serving his favorite enchiladas, "But I think it works. Grandpa says it works."

Fausto's ears perked up. That was the same kind the guy in Los Lobos played. Instead of asking for the guitar, he waited for his mother to offer it to him. And she did, while gathering the dishes from the table.

"No, Mom, I'll do it," he said, hugging her. "I'll do the dishes forever if you want."

It was the happiest day of his life. No, it was the second-happiest day of his life. The happiest was when his grandfather Lupe placed the *guitarron*, which was nearly as huge as a washtub, in his arms. Fausto ran a thumb down the strings, which vibrated in his throat and chest. It sounded beautiful, deep and eerie. A pumpkin smile widened on his face.

"Okay, *hijo*, now you put your fingers like this," said his grandfather, smelling of tobacco and aftershave. He took Fausto's fingers and placed them on the strings. Fausto strummed a chord on the *guitarron*, and the bass resounded in their chests.

The *guitarron* was more complicated than Fausto imagined. But he was confident that after a few more lessons he could start a band that would someday play on "American Bandstand" for the dancing crowds.

READING FOR UNDERSTANDING

1. What makes Fausto decide that his mission in life is to play the guitar?

2. What is the first thing Fausto decides to do to earn the money to buy a guitar?

3. How does he finally earn the money?

4. Why does Fausto feel guilty after he takes the dog to its home?

5. Why is Fausto happy at the end of the story?

RESPONDING TO THE STORY

Fausto is unhappy with his own behavior after he lies to the man and woman, and he feels unworthy of the money they gave him. To right the wrong, Fausto gives the money to charity. In a short paragraph, describe another way that you might have transformed Fausto's wrong into a right.

REVIEWING VOCABULARY

1. The rotation of the Earth is *perpetual,* or **(a)** backwards **(b)** continuous **(c)** very fast.

2. The jury was surprised by the criminal's *confession,* or **(a)** admission of guilt **(b)** refusal to speak **(c)** witty remark.

3. The first time she sang in public she knew she had found her life *mission,* or **(a)** education **(b)** calling **(c)** lesson.

4. *Empanada*s are fun to prepare because they are pastries made with a variety of **(a)** crusts **(b)** fillings **(c)** colors.

5. In a clear, loud voice, the *lector* at church **(a)** sweeps the floor **(b)** takes up the collection **(c)** reads the lesson.

THINKING CRITICALLY

1. Fausto wants a guitar so badly that he is willing to lie to get the money to buy one. Why do you think he changes his mind when the money is given to him?

2. Which of Fausto's later actions do you think shows that he is demonstrating personal responsibility?

WRITING PROJECTS

1. Write a scene in which Fausto returns to the dog's owners' house to tell them the truth and what he did with the money. Include the owners' reactions.

2. Imagine that you are Fausto at 20 years old. You now have a famous band and are being interviewed by a newspaper reporter. Write your answer to the reporter's question about how you came to play the *guitarron*.

THE PARABLE OF THE EAGLE

retold by Melissa Billings

Has anyone ever given you the advice, "Just be yourself"? No matter how people might try to control the way we act or feel, no one can change who we are on the inside. Because we may feel pressure to live up to the expectations of others, it takes confidence and inner strength to have the courage to be who we really are.

In this West African folktale, an eagle is raised to act like a chicken. A naturalist who knows that the bird is an eagle at heart doesn't give up until the eagle realizes it too.

VOCABULARY WORDS

naturalist (nach´ər əl ist) a person who studies nature
❖ The *naturalist* understands the behavior of animals.

soar (sôr) to fly high in the air
❖ We watched the hawk *soar* over the valley.

forth (fôrth) forward in place
❖ She stretched *forth* her hand for the mayor to shake.

screech (skrēch) a shrill, harsh sound
❖ The owl's *screech* startled the hikers.

mounted (mount´id) climbed
❖ The stunt plane *mounted* higher as the spectators watched.

content (kən tent´) satisfied
❖ I felt warm and *content* after the hearty meal.

 **A** **certain man went through a forest** seeking any bird of interest he might find. He caught a young eagle. Then he brought it home and put it among his fowls and ducks and turkeys. He gave it chicken food to eat, even though it was an eagle, the king of birds.

Five years later a naturalist came to see him and said, "That bird is an eagle, not a chicken."

"Yes," said its owner, "but I have trained it to be a chicken. It is no longer an eagle, even though it measures fifteen feet from tip to tip of its wings."

"No," said the naturalist, "it is an eagle still. It has the heart of an eagle, and I will make it soar high up to the heavens."

"No," said the owner, "it is a chicken, and it will never fly."

They agreed to test it. The naturalist picked up the eagle, held it up, and said, "Eagle, thou art an eagle. Thou dost belong to the sky and not to this earth. Stretch forth thy wings and fly!"

The eagle turned this way and that. Then, looking down, it saw the chickens eating their food and jumped down to join them.

The owner said, "I told you it was a chicken."

"No," said the naturalist, "it is an eagle. Give it another chance tomorrow."

So the next day he took it to the top of the house and said, "Eagle, thou art an eagle; stretch forth thy wings and fly!" But again the eagle, seeing the chickens feeding, jumped down and fed with them.

The owner said, "I told you it was a chicken."

"No," answered the naturalist, "it is an eagle, and it still has the heart of an eagle. Give it one more chance, and I will make it fly tomorrow."

The next morning he rose early and took the eagle outside the city, away from the houses, to the foot of a high mountain. The sun was just rising. Again he picked up the eagle and said to it, "Eagle, thou art an eagle. Thou dost belong to the sky and not of this earth. Stretch forth thy wings and fly!"

The eagle looked around and trembled as if new life were coming to it. But it did not fly. The naturalist made it look straight at the sun. Suddenly it stretched out its wings, and, with the screech of an eagle, it mounted higher and higher and never returned. It was an eagle, though it had been kept and tamed as a chicken!

My people of Africa, we were created in the image of God. But men have made us think that we are chickens, and we still think we are. But we are eagles. Stretch forth your wings and fly! Don't be content with the food of chickens!

READING FOR UNDERSTANDING

1. Why does the man believe that the eagle will never fly?

2. Why does the naturalist believe that the eagle *will* fly?

3. How many times does the naturalist try to make the eagle fly?

4. What does the naturalist say to the eagle each time he tries to make it fly?

5. Who is being addressed in the last paragraph of the story?

RESPONDING TO THE STORY

The eagle's owner thought it would never fly, but when the eagle realized what he truly was, he *was* able to fly. Write a paragraph describing the expectations you have of yourself and the steps that are necessary to achieve your goals.

REVIEWING VOCABULARY

Match each word in the left column with the correct definition in the right column.

1. mounted   **a.** a shrill, harsh sound

2. content   **b.** a person who studies nature

3. screech   **c.** climbed

4. naturalist   **d.** forward in place

5. forth   **e.** satisfied

THINKING CRITICALLY

1. Why do you think the eagle does not fly at the beginning of the folktale?

2. Why do you think the eagle does finally fly?

WRITING PROJECTS

1. In a journal entry, write your interpretation of the message that you think the narrator is sending in the last paragraph of the story.

2. Write a letter to your school principal nominating someone you know for "student of the month." Describe how that person demonstrates self-determination, and give examples of how he or she has overcome obstacles.

THE WOODEN SWORD

retold by Heather Forest

When circumstances in life change, it is sometimes hard to know what to do. Some people are able to see change as opportunity instead of as a disaster. They look for ways to make their lives better. They take the initiative by trying new jobs or new ways of living.

In this story, a worried, miserable king decides to find out how his subjects find happiness. The king encounters a poor but cheerful man who is always optimistic about life. The king believes that if the poor man's circumstances worsen, he will not remain cheerful. The king puts the man's positive attitude to several tests. How the poor man reacts to a series of changes is not what the king expects.

VOCABULARY WORDS

bazaar (bə zär´) a marketplace
❖ Many people are shopping at the *bazaar*.

dingy (din´jē) dirty-colored, not bright or clean
❖ The curtains I found in the attic were *dingy* and covered with dust.

quell (kwel) to put an end to
❖ The woman hoped to *quell* her fear of flying by reading about airplane safety.

furrowed (fŭr´ōd) deeply wrinkled
❖ His *furrowed* face shows how worried he is.

naive (nä ēv´) simple; childlike
❖ The girl was too *naive* to understand the complicated situation.

predicament (prē dik´ə mənt) a difficult situation
❖ The mischievous child cleverly gets out of his *predicament*.

sheath (shēth) a case for a knife or sword blade
❖ The blade's *sheath* is made of fine leather.

 **O**nce there was a king whose worrisome thoughts swirled around his head like a storm. He feared that his armies would lose battles. He fretted that his treasury would one day be empty. He suspected that his ministers were disloyal. He had no peace.

One day as the king stood at his window, gazing at the crowds in the marketplace beyond the palace walls, he wondered, "How do common people find happiness? Do they worry as much as I do?" He sighed and said to himself, "I wish I were a bird who could fly off and listen to their daily conversations."

Suddenly, the king's eyes brightened with an idea. He called his servants to bring him the crudest cloth they could find. He ordered royal seamstresses to assemble a suit of rags and a hooded cloak. When servants delivered these clothes to the royal chamber, the king sent everyone away and eyed the rough attire. Standing before the mirror, he carefully removed his crown, smudged his face with ashes, and dressed himself in the ragged clothes. He appeared every bit a beggar. Pleased with this disguise, he crept from the palace. Even the guards did not recognize him.

The disguised king walked freely through the crowds in the bazaar all day, observing the ways of common people. It was nightfall when he passed a run-down cottage at the edge of the city. Peeking through the window, the king saw a man sitting at a crude wooden table, eating a loaf of bread. The man's smile lit up the dingy room. The king eyed the meal and the humble surroundings. He wondered, "Why is this poor man so happy?" Unable to quell his curiosity, the king knocked on the door.

"I am a poor beggar," the king said in his humblest voice. "Can you spare some food?"

"Certainly!" said the poor man. "A guest is always a welcome blessing in this house. I do not have much, but what I have is yours."

The poor man's generosity dumbfounded the king. After the two seated themselves, the poor man piously blessed and cut the bread. The king accepted a share of the loaf and watched the man gaily chew the bread as if it were the finest meal.

"Why are you so happy?" the king asked.

The poor man replied, "It was a good day! I am a cobbler who repairs old shoes. Today I fixed enough shoes to earn a loaf of bread."

"But what if tomorrow you do not earn your bread?" the king inquired.

The poor man looked deep into the king's eyes. He saw how the strain of worry had furrowed his brow. The poor man smiled and simply replied, "Day by day, I have faith. All will be well."

The king mused over these words and thought to himself, "This man's faith brings him happiness. He is naive. I wonder how happy he would remain in times of difficulty."

The king left the cottage planning to test the man's faith.

The next morning when the man went out to ply his trade as a cobbler, he discovered the king had issued a new law. A large sign in the marketplace read, "It is henceforth illegal for anyone to repair shoes. When shoes wear out, people must buy new ones."

The poor man sighed and assured himself, "All will be well." He glanced about the market and noticed an old woman struggling with a bucket of water at the well. He rushed to assist her, and for his trouble, she handed him a coin. As the poor man fingered the coin in his hand, his faith in the future shone brightly. He carried water for people all day and by sunset had enough money to buy himself dinner.

Curious to see if his new friend could be happy without a meal, the king, again disguised as a beggar, returned to the poor man's house. To his surprise, through the window he saw the man eating bread and drinking a glass of wine.

He knocked on the door, and the poor man brought him immediately to the table. The king asked, "How is it that tonight you drink wine and eat bread? I have seen the new law posted in the market, so surely you did not fix shoes today!"

"No, indeed, I did not," explained the poor man. "Today I earned more than before by carrying water for people. The loss of my first profession has made room for my new one!"

"What if no one wants you to carry water tomorrow?" asked the king.

The poor man looked into the king's eyes and simply replied, "Day by day, I have faith. All will be well."

The king left the cottage, bewildered by the poor man's faith. "He has not tasted hard times," thought the king.

The next day when the poor man went to the well, he saw that the king had made yet another new law. The king's messengers posted a sign on the well: "It is now illegal for anyone to carry water for others."

The poor man considered this predicament for a moment and looked about the marketplace. He noticed men carrying wood from the forest on their backs. He approached a woodcutter and asked if he needed an assistant.

"Certainly!" was the reply, and the poor man spent the day cutting and carrying wood to market. By nightfall, he had earned enough to buy bread, wine, and cheese for his dinner.

When the king, again dressed as a beggar, arrived at the cottage, the poor man invited him to come inside.

To the king's surprise, the poor man shared an even finer meal.

"How did you earn your keep today?" inquired the king.

"I am a woodcutter now," said the poor man, smiling broadly. "As I told you, I have faith. As you can see, things are getting better all the time!"

The king grumbled as he left the cottage. "I must be far more clever in testing this man. Surely when he cannot buy food for his belly, his faith will waver."

The next day when the poor man went to join the other woodcutters, he found them surrounded by palace soldiers. The captain loudly announced, "The king has commanded that all woodcutters must report to the palace gate to become guards."

The captain shuffled the poor man off with the rest. The poor man, now dressed stiffly in a colorful uniform with a sharp sword in a sheath at his side, stood guard all day at the palace gate. As the sun set, he went to the captain of the soldiers to request some pay so that he could buy his evening meal.

"Palace guards are paid once a month," the captain curtly replied.

With a sigh, the poor man set out for home. As he passed the pawnshop, an idea came to him. He sold the metal blade of the sword for enough money to buy food for a month. "With what I earn by the end of the month as a guard," he thought, "I can easily buy back the sword and return it to its rightful place."

The poor man rushed home and set the table with a fine meal. Before he ate, however, he busied himself carving a wooden blade to fill the now empty sheath he would wear at his side the next day.

The king, once again disguised in rags, returned to the cottage and saw the food on the table. "How did you buy this food?" he asked in amazement, knowing that the man could not possibly have earned any money that day. The poor man explained, "I sold the metal blade of the sword for enough money to buy food for a month."

Never suspecting that the ragged beggar who stood before him was in fact the king, the poor man showed the wooden blade he was carving. "This will replace the blade I sold until I earn enough to buy it back again."

"That is not so clever of you," said the king. "What if you must draw your sword tomorrow?"

Once again the poor man replied, "Day by day, I have faith. All will be well."

"I have him now!" the king chuckled under his breath as he left the cottage. "His faith will not be so strong in the dungeon!"

The next day the poor man stood in uniform once again, guarding the palace gate. The captain of the king's soldiers, followed by a noisy crowd, dragged a man accused of being a thief. The captain led the thief up to the poor man at the palace gate and gruffly said, "This thief has stolen a melon. The king has ordered you to cut off his head immediately."

The thief begged for mercy. He fell to his knees, weeping. "Please do not kill me! I had no food and my children were hungry."

The poor man, guarding the gate, stood tall in his uniform and calmly considered the awkward situation. He thought, "If I pull out my sword to kill this man, I, too, will be beheaded. Everyone will see that the royal blade is missing!" He pondered a bit more and then solemnly reminded himself, "All will be well."

As the large crowd watched, he lifted his arms to the heavens and cried out, "Blessed be the Most High! If this man is truly guilty, give me the strength to serve the king's command. But if this man is innocent," he said, gripping the handle of the sword at his side, "let the blade of my sword be turned to wood!"

Dramatically, he drew his wooden sword and thrust it high above his head. A gasp went through the crowd. "It's a miracle!" people exclaimed. Immediately, the man accused of theft was set free.

At that moment, out of the crowd stepped the king. He approached the poor man in the guard uniform and said, "Do you recognize me?"

The man replied, "You are the king."

"No," replied the king, "I am the beggar whom you fed each night."

The poor man's face spread with a smile, for he recognized the king's furrowed brow.

The king smiled in return and said, "Tonight and every night, my friend, you will dine with me! Your light of faith can help me chase away my dark fears of the future."

And so it came to pass that the man, who owned little but was rich in faith, became the wise and trusted adviser to the king.

READING FOR UNDERSTANDING

1. How does the king try to deal with his worries?

2. Why does the king wish that he were a bird?

3. What does the king do to disguise himself?

4. What does the poor man do when the king knocks on his door?

5. How does the king test the poor man?

RESPONDING TO THE STORY

In spite of his problems, the poor man improves his situation because of his optimistic outlook on life and his willingness to adapt to new circumstances. In a short paragraph, describe someone you know or have heard or read about who has made the most of a change in circumstances.

REVIEWING VOCABULARY

Match each word on the left with the correct definition on the right.

1. predicament   **a.** simple; childlike

2. quell   **b.** dirty-colored

3. naive   **c.** deeply wrinkled

4. furrowed   **d.** a difficult situation

5. dingy   **e.** put an end to

THINKING CRITICALLY

1. Why do you think the poor man remained optimistic?

2. Do you think the king will become less worried? Why or why not?

WRITING PROJECTS

1. Write a speech praising the positive aspects of an optimistic outlook.

2. Imagine a scene where the poor man advises the king. Describe what the poor man might have said.

THE RICHER, THE POORER

by Dorothy West

How people define wealth is influenced by what they consider important in life. One person may think that being wealthy means having an abundance of money and possessions. Another person may regard access to books and ideas as a form of wealth. Still another might say that the greatest riches in life are friends and family and love.

In Dorothy West's short story "The Richer, the Poorer," two women, now in their sixties, have viewed life and wealth in very different ways. They come together after having lived separately since becoming adults. They both realize that they still have a lot to learn about themselves and what's important in life.

VOCABULARY WORDS

mean (mēn) small-minded; petty and selfish
❖ Mildred regretted living such a *mean* life.

abroad (ə brôd´) outside one's own country
❖ I hope to study *abroad* during college.

frugally (froo´gəl ē) thriftily; not wastefully
❖ The shopkeeper lived *frugally* to save for his
retirement.

beau (bō) a girl's or woman's sweetheart
❖ Michele's new *beau* brought her flowers.

miserly (mī´zər lē) greedy; stingy
❖ Our neighbor was too *miserly* to buy anyone a gift.

threadbare (thred´ber´) shabby; worn down
❖ The sofa is so old that it is nearly *threadbare*.

enhanced (en hanst´) improved; increased in value
❖ The elderly woman *enhanced* her life by doing
volunteer work.

giddy (gid´ē) lightheaded; dizzy
❖ Margaret was *giddy* with excitement when she won
the contest.

**O**ver the years Lottie had urged Bess to prepare for her old age. Over the years Bess had lived each day as if there were no other. Now they were both past sixty, the time for summing up. Lottie had a bank account that had never grown lean. Bess had the clothes on her back and the rest of her worldly possessions in a battered suitcase.

Lottie had hated being a child, hearing her parents' skimping and scraping. Bess had never seemed to notice. All she ever wanted was to go outside and play. She learned to skate on borrowed skates. She rode a borrowed bicycle. Lottie couldn't wait to grow up and buy herself the best of everything.

As soon as anyone would hire her, Lottie put herself to work. She minded babies; she ran errands for the old.

She never touched a penny of her money, though her child's mouth watered for ice cream and candy. But she could not bear to share with Bess, who never had anything to share with her. When the dimes began to add up to dollars, she lost her taste for sweets.

By the time she was twelve, she was clerking after school in a small variety store. Saturdays she worked as long as she was wanted. She decided to keep her money for clothes. When she entered high school, she would wear a wardrobe that neither she nor anyone else would be able to match.

But her freshman year found her unable to indulge so frivolous a whim, particularly when her admiring instructors advised her to think seriously of college. No one in her family had ever gone to college, and certainly Bess would never get there. She would show them all what she could do if she put her mind to it.

She began to bank her money, and her bank became her most private and precious possession.

In her third year of high school she found a job in a small but expanding restaurant, where she cashiered from the busy hour until closing. In her last year of high school the business increased so rapidly that Lottie was faced with the choice of staying in school or working full time.

She made her choice easily. A job in hand was worth two in the future.

Bess had a beau in the school band, who had no other ambition except to play a horn. Lottie expected to be settled with a home and family while Bess was still waiting for Harry to earn enough to buy a marriage license.

That Bess married Harry straight out of high school was not surprising. That Lottie never married at all was not really surprising either. Two or three times she was halfway persuaded, but to give up a job that paid well for a homemaking job that paid nothing was a risk she was incapable of taking.

Bess's married life was nothing for Lottie to envy. She and Harry lived like gypsies, Harry playing in second-rate bands all over the country, even getting himself and Bess stranded in Europe. They were often in rags and never in riches.

Bess grieved because she had no child, not having sense enough to know she was better off without one. Lottie was certainly better off without nieces and nephews to feel sorry for. Very likely Bess would have dumped them on her doorstep.

That Lottie had a doorstep they might have been left on was only because her boss, having bought a second house, offered Lottie his first house at a price so low and terms so reasonable that it would have been like losing money to refuse.

She shut off the rooms she didn't use, letting them go to rack and ruin. Since she ate her meals out, she had no food at home and did not encourage callers, who always expected a cup of tea.

Her way of life was mean and miserly, but she did not know it. She thought she lived frugally in her middle years so that she could live in comfort and ease when she most needed peace of mind.

The years, after forty, began to race. Suddenly Lottie was sixty, and retired from her job by her boss's son, who had no sentimental feeling about keeping her on until she was ready to quit.

She made several attempts to find other employment, but her dowdy appearance made her look old and inefficient. For the first time in her life Lottie would have gladly worked for nothing to have some place to go, something to do with her day.

Harry died abroad, in a third-rate hotel, with Bess weeping as hard as if he had left her a fortune. He had left her nothing but his horn. There wasn't even money for her passage home.

Lottie, trapped by the blood tie, knew she would not only have to send for her sister but take her in when she returned. It didn't seem fair that Bess should reap the harvest of Lottie's lifetime of self-denial.

It took Lottie a week to get a bedroom ready, a week of hard work and hard cash. There was everything to do, everything to replace or paint. When she was through, the room looked so fresh and new that Lottie felt she deserved it more than Bess.

She would let Bess have her room, but the mattress was so lumpy, the carpet so worn, the curtains so threadbare that Lottie's conscience pricked her. She supposed she would have to redo that room, too, and went about doing it with an eagerness that she mistook for haste.

When she was through upstairs, she was shocked to see how dismal downstairs looked by comparison. She tried to ignore it, but with nowhere to go to escape it, the contrast grew more intolerable.

She worked her way from kitchen to parlor, persuading herself she was only putting the rooms to rights to give herself something to do. At night she slept like a child after a long and happy day of playing house. She was having more fun than she had ever had in her life. She was living each hour for itself.

There was only a day now before Bess would arrive. Passing her gleaming mirrors, at first with vague awareness, then with painful clarity, Lottie saw herself as others saw her and could not stand the sight.

She went on a spending spree from the specialty shops to beauty salon, emerging transformed into a woman who believed in miracles.

She was in the kitchen basting a turkey when Bess rang the bell. Her heart raced, and she wondered if the heat from the oven was responsible.

She went to the door, and Bess stood before her. Stiffly she suffered Bess's embrace, her heart racing harder, her eyes suddenly smarting from the onrush of cold air.

"Oh, Lottie, it's good to see you," Bess said, but saying nothing about Lottie's splendid appearance. Upstairs Bess, putting down her shabby suitcase, said, "I'll sleep like a rock tonight," without a word of praise for her lovely room. At the lavish table, top-heavy with turkey, Bess said, "I'll take light and dark both," with no marveling at the size of the bird or that there was turkey for two elderly women, one of them too poor to buy her own bread.

With the glow of good food in her stomach, Bess began to spin stories. They were rich with places and people, most of them lowly, all of them magnificent.

Her face reflected her telling, the joys and sorrows of her remembering, and above all, the love she lived by that enhanced the poorest place, the humblest person.

Then it was that Lottie knew why Bess had made no mention of her finery, or the shining room, or the twelve-pound turkey. She had not even seen them. Tomorrow she would see the place as it really looked, and Lottie as she really looked, and the warmed-over turkey in its second-day glory. Today she saw only what she had come seeking, a place in her sister's home and heart.

She said, "That's enough about me. How have the years used you?"

"It was me who didn't use them," said Lottie wistfully. "I saved for them. I saved for them. I forgot the best of them would go without my ever spending a day or a dollar enjoying them. That's my life story in those few words, a life never lived.

"Now it's too near the end to try."

Bess said, "To know how much there is to know is the beginning of learning to live. Don't count the years that are left us. At our time of life it's the days that count. You've too much catching up to do to waste a minute of a waking hour feeling sorry for yourself."

Lottie grinned, a real wide-open grin. "Well to tell the truth, I felt sorry for you. Maybe if I had any sense I'd feel sorry for myself, after all. I know I'm too old to kick up my heels, but I'm going to let you show me how. If I land on my head, I guess it won't matter; I feel giddy already, and I like it."

READING FOR UNDERSTANDING

1. How are Lottie and Bess related?

2. Why did Lottie never get married?

3. What became Lottie's most private and precious possession?

4. How did Bess get the money to return home when her husband died?

5. Why did Lottie finally spend money to improve her house?

RESPONDING TO THE STORY

Lottie spent her life saving for the future while Bess lived her life for each moment. Think about the positive and negative aspects of each of their lives. Then make a list of the pros and cons of each lifestyle.

REVIEWING VOCABULARY

1. The woman is *miserly*; she refuses to **(a)** live alone **(b)** spend money **(c)** work.

2. Jana lives *frugally* by **(a)** spending little money **(b)** taking time to make decisions **(c)** buying whatever she wants.

3. Her furniture is *threadbare*, which means that it is **(a)** fancy **(b)** new **(c)** shabby.

4. The flavor of the food was *enhanced* by **(a)** being overcooked **(b)** the delicious spices **(c)** the menu.

5. While the professor lived *abroad*; she lived **(a)** in another country **(b)** in a suburb **(c)** in a rural area.

THINKING CRITICALLY

1. Lottie had always thought of herself as smarter, happier, richer, and more sensible than Bess. What new knowledge of herself does Lottie gain after Bess arrives?

2. If you had to choose to live like either Lottie or Bess, which one's life would you choose, and why?

WRITING PROJECTS

1. Write a new ending to the story that shows what might have happened if Lottie had gone to live with Bess.

2. Write a journal entry about what you believe is most important in life.

KUPTI AND IMANI

retold by Andrew Lang

Do you prefer the safety of being cared for or would you rather go out on your own? Some people are eager to take on the world and to rely only on themselves and their own abilities.

In this story, a king asks his two daughters if they would be satisfied leaving their lives and fortunes in his hands. One daughter, Kupti, says she will be glad to do so. The other, Imani, says she wants to make her own fortune. The king is displeased with her answer and, as punishment, sends her to live with an impoverished fakir, or beggar. In this Indian legend, Princess Imani proves to everyone that she is as capable of caring for herself as she says she is.

VOCABULARY WORDS

fakir (fə kir´) a Muslim or Hindu beggar
* ❖ The *fakir* lived on what he was given by other people.

perplexity (pər pleks´ə tē) confusion
* ❖ The student's *perplexity* was from not knowing how to solve the problem.

loom (lo͞om) a machine for weaving thread into cloth
* ❖ The brightly colored cloth was woven on a *loom*.

flax (flaks) plant fibers that are spun into linen thread
* ❖ Many plants, such as *flax* and cotton, produce fibers that are used for cloth.

casket (kas´kit) a small box
* ❖ The boy collected insects in a wooden *casket*.

agony (ag´ə nē) extreme pain or distress
* ❖ The accident victim screamed in *agony*.

signet (sig´nit) a seal used as a signature
* ❖ The ring contains a *signet* in the form of an initial.

Once there was a king who had two daughters and their names were Kupti and Imani. He loved them both very much and spent hours in talking to them. One day he said to Kupti, the elder:

"Are you satisfied to leave your life and fortune in my hands?"

"Verily, yes," answered the princess, surprised at the question. "In whose hands should I leave them, if not in yours?"

But when he asked his younger daughter Imani the same question, she replied:

"No, indeed! If I had the chance I would make my own fortune."

At this answer the king was very displeased and said, "You are too young to know the meaning of your words. But, be it so, my daughter, I will give you the chance of gratifying your wish."

Then he sent for an old lame *fakir* who lived in a tumble-down hut on the outskirts of the city, and when he had presented himself, the king said:

"No doubt, as you are very old and nearly crippled, you would be glad to have some young person live with you and serve you; so I will send you my younger daughter. She wants to earn her living and she can do so with you."

Of course the old *fakir* had not a word to say, or if he had, he was really too astonished and troubled to say it. But the young princess went off with him smiling and tripped along quite gaily, while he hobbled home with her in perplexed silence.

As soon as they reached the hut, the *fakir* began to think what he could arrange for the princess's comfort. But after all he was a *fakir*, and his house was bare except for one bedstead, two old cooking pots, and an earthen jar for water, and one cannot get much comfort out of such things. However, the princess soon ended his perplexity by asking:

"Have you any money?"

"I have a penny somewhere," replied the *fakir*.

"Very well," rejoined the princess, "give me the penny and go out and borrow me a spinning wheel and a loom."

After much seeking the *fakir* found the penny and started on his errand, while the princess went shopping. First she bought a farthing's worth of oil, and then she bought three farthings' worth of flax. When she returned with her purchases she set the old man on the bedstead and rubbed his crippled leg with the oil for an hour.

Then she sat down at the spinning wheel and spun and spun all night long while the old man slept. In the morning, she had spun the finest thread that ever was seen. Next she went to the loom and wove and wove until by evening she had woven a beautiful silver cloth.

"Now," said she to the *fakir*, "go into the market place and sell my cloth while I rest."

"And what am I to ask for it?" said the old man.

"Two gold pieces," replied the princess.

So the *fakir* hobbled away and stood in the market place to sell the cloth. Presently the elder princess drove by, and when she saw the cloth she stopped and asked the price, for it was better work than she or any of her women could weave.

"Two gold pieces," said the *fakir*. And the princess gladly paid them, after which the old *fakir* hobbled home with the money.

As she had done before so Imani did again day after day. Always she spent a penny upon oil and flax, always she tended the old man's lame leg and spun and wove the most beautiful cloths and sold them at high prices. Gradually the city became famous for her beautiful stuffs, the old *fakir's* lame leg became straighter and stronger, and the hole under the floor of the hut where they kept their money became fuller and fuller of gold pieces. At last, one day, the princess said:

"I really think we have enough to live on in greater comfort." She sent for builders, and they built a beautiful house for her and the old *fakir*, and in all the city there was none finer except for the king's palace. Presently this reached the ears of the king, and when he inquired whose it was they told him that it belonged to his daughter.

"Well," exclaimed the king, "she said that she would make her own fortune, and somehow or other she seems to have done it!"

A little while after this, business took the king to another country, and before he went he asked his elder daughter what she would like him to bring her back as a gift.

"A necklace of rubies," answered she. And then the king thought he would like to ask Imani, too; so he sent a messenger to find out what sort of present she wanted. The man happened to arrive just as she was trying to disentangle a knot in her loom, and bowing low before her, he said:

"The king sends me to inquire what you wish him to bring you as a present from the country of Dûr?" But Imani, who was only considering how she could best untie the knot without breaking the thread, replied:

"Patience," meaning that the messenger should wait till she was able to attend to him. But the messenger went off with this as an answer and told the king that the only thing Princess Imani wanted was patience.

"Oh!" said the king. "I don't know whether that's a thing to be bought at Dûr. I never had it myself, but if it is to be found I will buy it for her."

Next day the king departed on his journey, and when

his business at Dûr was completed he bought for Kupti a beautiful ruby necklace. Then he said to a servant:

"The Princess Imani wants some patience. I did not know there was such a thing, but you must go to the market and inquire, and if any is to be sold, get it and bring it to me."

The servant saluted and left the king's presence. He walked about the market for some time crying, "Has anyone patience to sell? Patience to sell?" And some of the people mocked, and some, who had no patience, told him to go away and not be a fool, and some said, "The fellow's mad! As though one could buy or sell patience!"

At length it came to the ears of the King of Dûr that a madman was in the market trying to buy patience. The king laughed and said:

"I should like to see that fellow; bring him here!"

And immediately his attendants went to seek the man and brought him to the king, who asked, "What is this you want?"

And the man replied, "Sire, I am bidden to ask for patience."

"Oh," said the king, "you must have a strange master! What does he want with it?"

"My master wants it as a present for his daughter Imani," replied the servant.

"Well," said the king, "I know of some patience which the young lady might have if she cares for it, but it is not to be bought."

Now the king's name was Subbar Khan, and Subbar means patience; but the messenger did not know that, or understand that he was making a joke. However, he declared that Princess Imani was not only young and beautiful, but also the cleverest, most industrious, and kindest-hearted of princesses. And he would have gone on explaining her virtues had not the king laughingly put up his hand and stopped him, saying: "Well, well, wait a minute, and I will see what can be done."

With that he rose and went to his own apartments and took out a little casket. Into the casket he put a fan, and shutting it up carefully, he brought it to the messenger and said:

"Here is a casket. It has neither lock nor key and yet will open only to the touch of the person who needs its contents—and whoever opens it will obtain patience; but I cannot tell whether it will be the kind of patience that is wanted."

The servant bowed low and took the casket, but when he asked what was to be paid, the king would take nothing. So he went away and gave the casket and an account of his adventures to his master.

As soon as their father returned to his country, Kupti and Imani each received the presents he had brought for them. Imani was very surprised when the casket was brought to her by the hand of a messenger.

"But," she said, "what is this? I never asked for anything! Indeed I had no time, for the messenger ran away before I had unraveled my tangle."

But the servant declared the casket was for her, so she took it with some curiosity and brought it to the old *fakir*. The old man tried to open it, but in vain—so closely did the lid fit that it seemed to be quite immovable, and yet there was neither lock nor bolt nor spring, nor anything apparently by which the casket was kept shut. When he was tired of trying he handed the casket to the princess, who hardly touched it before it opened quite easily, and there lay within a beautiful fan. With a cry of surprise and pleasure Imani took out the fan and began to fan herself.

Hardly had she finished three strokes of the fan before there suddenly appeared before her King Subbar Khan of Dûr! The princess gasped and rubbed her eyes, and the old *fakir* sat and gazed in such astonishment that for some minutes he could not speak. At length he said:

"Who may you be, fair sir, if you please?"

"My name," said the king, "is Subbar Khan of Dûr. This lady," bowing to the princess, "has summoned me, and here I am!"

"I?" stammered the princess. "I have summoned you? I never saw or heard of you in my life before, so how could that be?"

Then the king told them how he had heard of a man in his own city of Dûr trying to buy patience, and how he had given him the fan in the casket. "Both are magical," he added. "When anyone uses the fan, in three strokes of it I am with her; if she folds it and taps it on the table, in three taps I am at home again. The casket will not open to all, but you see it was this fair lady who asked for patience, and as that is my name, here I am, very much at her service."

Now Princess Imani, being of a high spirit, was anxious to fold up the fan and give it the three taps which would send the king home again. But the old *fakir* was very pleased with his guest, and so in one way and another they spent a pleasant evening together before Subbar Khan took his leave.

After that he was often summoned, and as both the *fakir* and he were very fond of chess and were good players, they used to sit up half the night playing, and at last a little room in the house began to be called the king's room. Whenever he stayed late he used to sleep there and go home again in the morning.

By-and-by it came to the ears of Princess Kupti that a rich and handsome young man was visiting her sister's house, and she was very jealous. So she went one day to pay Imani a visit, pretending to be very affectionate and interested in the house, and in the way in which

Imani and the old *fakir* lived, and of their mysterious and royal visitor.

As the sisters went from place to place, Kupti was shown Subbar Khan's room; and presently, making some excuse, she slipped in by herself and swiftly spread under the sheet which lay upon the bed a quantity of very finely powdered and splintered glass which was poisoned, and which she had brought with her concealed in her clothes. Shortly afterward she took leave of her sister, declaring she could never forgive herself for not having come near her all this time, and that she would now begin to make amends for her neglect.

That very evening Subbar Khan came and sat up late with the old *fakir* playing chess as usual. Very tired, he at length bade him and the princess good night and, as soon as he lay down on the bed, thousands of tiny, tiny splinters of poisoned glass ran into him. He could not think what was the matter, and turned this way and that until he was pricked all over and felt as though he were burning from head to foot. But he never said a word, only sitting up all night in an agony of body and in worse agony of mind to think he should have been poisoned, as he guessed he was, in Imani's own house.

In the morning, although he was nearly fainting, he still said nothing, and by means of the magic fan was duly transported home again. Then he sent for all the physicians and doctors in his kingdom, but none could make out what his illness was. And so he lingered on for weeks and weeks, trying every remedy that anyone could devise, and passing sleepless nights and days of pain and fever and misery, until at last he was at the point of death.

Meanwhile Princess Imani and the old *fakir* were much troubled because, although they waved the magic fan again and again, no Subbar Khan appeared, and they feared that he had tired of them, or that some evil fate had overtaken him. At last the princess was in such a miserable state of doubt and uncertainty that she determined to go herself to the kingdom of Dûr and see what was the matter. Disguising herself as a young *fakir*, she set out upon her journey alone and on foot, as a *fakir* should travel.

One evening she found herself in a forest and lay down under a great tree to pass the night. But she could not sleep for thinking of Subbar Khan and wondering what had happened to him. Presently she heard two great monkeys talking to each other in the tree above her head.

"Good evening, brother," said one, "whence come you and what is the news?"

"I come from Dûr," said the other, "and the news is that the king is dying."

"Oh," said the first, "I'm sorry to hear that, for he is a master hand at slaying leopards and creatures that ought not to be allowed to live. What is the matter with him?"

"No man knows," replied the second monkey, "but the birds, who see all and carry all messages, say that he is dying of poisoned glass that Kupti the king's daughter spread upon his bed."

"Ah," said the first monkey, "that is sad news. But if they only knew it, the berries of the very tree we sit in, steeped in hot water, will cure such a disease as that in three days at most."

"True!" said the other. "It is a pity we cannot tell some man of a medicine so simple and so save a good man's life. But men are so silly; they go and shut themselves up in stuffy houses in stuffy cities instead of living in nice airy trees, and so they miss knowing all the best things."

Now when Imani heard that Subbar Khan was dying she began to weep silently, but as she listened she dried her tears and sat up, and as soon as daylight dawned over the forest she began to gather the berries from the

tree until she had filled her cloth with a load of them.
Then she walked on as fast as she could, and in two
days reached the city of Dûr. The first thing she did was
to pass through the market crying:

"Medicine for sale! Are any ill that need my
medicine?"

And presently one man said to his neighbor, "See,
there is a young *fakir* with medicine for sale, perhaps
he could do something for the king."

"Pooh," replied the other, "where so many graybeards
have failed, how should a lad like that be of any use?"

"Still," said the first, "he might try." And he went up
and spoke to Imani, and together they set out for the
palace and announced that another doctor was come to
try and cure the king.

After some delay Imani was admitted to the sick
room, and, while she was so well disguised that the
king did not recognize her, he was so wasted by illness
that she hardly knew him. But she began at once, full
of hope, by asking for some apartment all to herself
and a pot in which to boil water.

As soon as the water was heated, she steeped some of
her berries in it and, giving the mixture to the king's
attendants, told them to wash his body with it. The first
washing did so much good that the king slept quietly all
night. Again, the second day, she did the same, and this
time the king declared he was hungry and called for
food. After the third day he was quite well, only very
weak from his long illness. On the fourth day he got up
and sat upon his throne, and then sent messengers to
fetch the physician who had cured him.

When Imani appeared everyone marveled that so young
a man should be so clever a doctor, and the king wanted
to give him immense presents of money and all kinds of
precious things. At first Imani would take nothing, but at
last she said that, if she must be rewarded, she would

ask for the king's signet ring and his handkerchief. So, as she would take nothing more, the king gave her his signet ring and his handkerchief, and she departed and traveled back to her own country as fast as she could.

A little while after her return, when she had related to the *fakir* all her adventures, they sent for Subbar Khan by means of the magic fan, and when he appeared they asked him why he had stayed away for so long. Then he told them all about his illness and how he had been cured, and when he had finished, the princess rose up and, opening a cabinet, brought out the ring and the handkerchief and said, laughing:

"Are these the rewards you gave to your doctor?"

At that the king recognized her and understood in a moment all that had happened, and he jumped up and put the magic fan in his pocket, declaring that no one should send him away to his own country any more unless Imani would come with him and be his wife. And so it was settled, and the old *fakir* and Imani went to the city of Dûr, where Imani was married to the king and lived happily ever after.

READING FOR UNDERSTANDING

1. What happens when the younger sister refuses her father's offer to manage her fortune?

2. What does Imani tell the *fakir* to borrow?

3. Why does Imani want oil?

4. What does the messenger think that Imani wants her father to bring her from Dûr?

5. What heals Subbar Khan?

RESPONDING TO THE STORY

Imani could have had everything she could ever need or want provided for her and would not have had to work or make any decisions. Do you know or have you heard or read about someone else who turned down a lifestyle such as this in order to rely only on himself or herself? In a short paragraph, explain what he or she did to demonstrate self-reliance.

REVIEWING VOCABULARY

Fill in each blank with the correct word from the following list: *signet, loom, casket, agony, perplexity*.

1. A small box may be called a _____ .

2. A person who is in great pain is said to be in

_____ .

3. The word *confusion* means the same as the word

_____ .

4. A seal used as a signature is a _____ .

5. A machine called a _____ is used for weaving thread into cloth.

THINKING CRITICALLY

1. The king offers to take charge of Imani's life and fortune. Make a list of reasons why a person might say no to such an offer.

2. What does Imani do after she leaves home that shows that she is self-reliant? List the events in the order that they occur in the legend.

WRITING PROJECTS

1. Write one paragraph contrasting Kupti and Imani. Consider their reliance on self or others, their treatment of other people, and what each considers important in life.

2. Write a dialogue between Kupti and Imani where they discuss the decisions they made about their fortunes.

HELEN KELLER AND ANNE SULLIVAN

excerpted from *The Story of My Life*

In 1880, a girl was born to Kate and Arthur Keller of Tuscumbia, Alabama. When the child, Helen, was one year old, she became ill with a high fever that left her deaf and blind. Medical science could do nothing for her, but eventually a doctor suggested that the Kellers send for a teacher from Perkins Institution for the Blind, in Boston.

Anne Sullivan, Helen's teacher, worked with her for the next 49 years, during some of which time Helen was formally educated and graduated from Radcliffe College. Helen Keller then dedicated her life to helping people with physical challenges. In spite of her inability to see or hear, she became an inspiring writer, speaker, advocate, and fund-raiser. The patience and persistence of both Anne Sullivan and Helen Keller changed Helen's life from one of frustration to one of triumph. This autobiographical account tells how it all began.

VOCABULARY WORDS

dumb (dum) lacking the ability to speak

❖ She was so shocked by the question, that she was temporarily struck *dumb*.

languor (lang´gər) a lack of spirit or interest

❖ The horse's deep *languor* concerned the veterinarian.

tangible (tan´jə bəl) able to be felt; having actual form

❖ The tension in the air seemed *tangible*.

plummet (plum´it) a lead weight hung at the end of a line, used to determine depth

❖ The sailor used the sounding line and *plummet* to make sure that the boat would not run aground.

compass (kum´pəs) an instrument that indicates direction

❖ The *compass* shows that the ship is traveling northeast.

tussle (tus´əl) a struggle

❖ The brothers had a *tussle* over who would get the last piece of cake.

confounding (kən found´ing) confusing

❖ I kept *confounding* the rules of the game.

dashed (dasht) threw so as to break

❖ He *dashed* the plate against the wall in a fit of anger.

The most important day I remember in all my life is the one on which my teacher, Anne Mansfield Sullivan, came to me. I am filled with wonder when I consider the immeasurable contrasts between the two lives which it connects. It was the third of March, 1887, three months before I was seven years old.

On the afternoon of that eventful day, I stood on the porch, dumb and expectant. I guessed vaguely from my mother's signs and from the hurrying to and fro in the house that something unusual was about to happen, so I went to the door and waited on the steps. The afternoon sun penetrated the mass of honeysuckle that covered the porch, and fell on my upturned face. My fingers lingered almost unconsciously on the familiar leaves and blossoms which had just come forth to greet the sweet southern spring. I did not know what the future held of marvel or surprise for me. Anger and bitterness had preyed upon me continually for weeks, and a deep languor had succeeded this passionate struggle.

Have you ever been at sea in a dense fog, when it seemed as if a tangible white darkness shut you in, and the great ship, tense and anxious, groped her way toward the shore with plummet and sounding-line and you waited with beating heart for something to happen? I was like that ship before my education began, only I was without compass or sounding-line, and had no way of knowing how near the harbor was. "Light! Give me light!" was the wordless cry of my soul, and the light of love shone on me in that very hour. I felt approaching footsteps. I stretched out my hand as I supposed to my mother. Some one took it, and I was caught up and held close in the arms of her who had come to reveal all things to me and, more than all things else, to love me.

The morning after my teacher came, she led me into her room and gave me a doll. The little blind children at the Perkins Institution had sent it and Laura Bridgman had dressed it, but I did not know this until afterward. When I had played with it a little while, Miss Sullivan slowly spelled into my hand the word "d-o-l-l." I was at once interested in this finger play and tried to imitate it. When I finally succeeded in making the letters correctly I was flushed with childish pleasure and pride. Running downstairs to my mother I held up my hand and made the letters for doll. I did not know that I was spelling a word or even that words existed; I was simply making my fingers go in monkey-like imitation. In the days that followed I learned to spell in this uncomprehending way a great many words, among them *pin*, *hat*, *cup*, and a few verbs like *sit*, *stand*, and *walk*. But my teacher had been with me several weeks before I understood that everything has a name.

One day, while I was playing with my new doll, Miss Sullivan put my big rag doll into my lap also, spelled "d-o-l-l" and tried to make me understand that "d-o-l-l" applied to both. Earlier in the day we had had a tussle over the words "m-u-g" and "w-a-t-e-r." Miss Sullivan had tried to impress it upon me that "m-u-g" is *mug* and that "w-a-t-e-r" is *water*, but I persisted in confounding the two. In despair she had dropped the subject for the time, only to renew it at the first opportunity. I became impatient at her repeated attempts and, seizing the new doll, I dashed it upon the floor. I was keenly delighted when I felt the fragments of the broken doll at my feet. Neither sorrow nor regret followed my passionate outburst. I had not loved the doll. In the still, dark world in which I lived there was no strong sentiment or tenderness. I felt my teacher

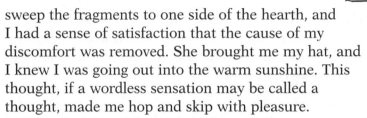

sweep the fragments to one side of the hearth, and
I had a sense of satisfaction that the cause of my
discomfort was removed. She brought me my hat, and
I knew I was going out into the warm sunshine. This
thought, if a wordless sensation may be called a
thought, made me hop and skip with pleasure.

We walked down the path to the well-house, attracted
by the fragrance of the honeysuckle with which it was
covered. Someone was drawing water and my teacher
placed my hand under the spout. As the cool stream
gushed over one hand she spelled into the other the
word *water*, first slowly, then rapidly. I stood still, my
whole attention fixed upon the motions of her fingers.
Suddenly I felt a misty consciousness as of something
forgotten—a thrill of returning thought, and somehow
the mystery of language was revealed to me. I knew
then that "w-a-t-e-r" meant the wonderful cool
something that was flowing over my hand. That living
word awakened my soul, gave it light, hope, joy, set it
free! There were barriers still, it is true, but barriers
that could in time be swept away.

I left the well-house eager to learn. Everything had a
name, and each name gave birth to a new thought. As
we returned to the house every object which I touched
seemed to quiver with life. That was because I saw
everything with the strange, new sight that had come to
me. On entering the door I remembered the doll I had
broken. I felt my way to the hearth and picked up the
pieces. I tried vainly to put them together. Then my
eyes filled with tears; for I realized what I had done,
and for the first time I felt repentance and sorrow.

I learned a great many new words that day. I do not
remember what they all were, but I do know that
mother, *father*, *sister*, and *teacher* were among them—
words that were to make the world blossom for me,
"like Aaron's rod, with flowers." It would have been

difficult to find a happier child than I was as I lay in my crib at the close of that eventful day and lived over the joys it had brought me and for the first time longed for a new day to come.

READING FOR UNDERSTANDING

1. What physical obstacles does Helen Keller have to overcome?

2. How did Helen Keller feel at the beginning of the selection?

3. Who is Anne Sullivan?

4. What concept does Anne Sullivan teach Helen besides words?

5. How does Anne Sullivan teach words to Helen?

RESPONDING TO THE STORY

Anne Sullivan shows great patience and persistence in reaching Helen. Helen herself exhibits these same character traits later in her life. Do you know or have you read or heard about someone else who has possessed these traits? In a short paragraph, discuss how he or she showed great patience and persistence.

REVIEWING VOCABULARY

1. The *tussle* the players had was quite a **(a)** pleasure **(b)** speech **(c)** struggle.

2. If a person is *dumb*, he or she is unable to **(a)** speak **(b)** walk **(c)** learn.

3. If Eli is *confounding* two concepts, he is **(a)** separating them **(b)** confusing them **(c)** analyzing them.

4. If something is *tangible*, it can be **(a)** touched **(b)** heard **(c)** learned.

5. A person experiencing *languor* lacks **(a)** food **(b)** spirit **(c)** shelter.

65

THINKING CRITICALLY

1. Anne Sullivan shows patience in this selection. She does not give up on Helen even when Helen is angry and impatient and does not cooperate. How does the selection show Anne's persistence?

2. Why is Helen Keller so happy about learning the word *water*?

WRITING PROJECTS

1. Imagine that you are one of Helen's parents. Write a letter to a relative that reveals how you feel about the changes in Helen since Anne Sullivan's arrival.

2. Pretend you are Anne Sullivan and write a letter to a friend describing your teaching of Helen Keller. Focus on the way you relied on patience and persistence to get through to her.

"No man is an island, entire of itself." — John Donne

Unit 2
REACHING OUT

DAMON AND PYTHIAS

retold by Louis Untermeyer

Many of us have friends whom we help out, play with, and trust with our secrets. We depend on these friends for fun, companionship, and support. But how many of us would be willing to risk our lives for our best friend?

Damon and Pythias are best friends. When Pythias is punished by Dionysius, the ruler of Syracuse, Damon unhesitatingly takes his friend's place—even though it means he will be punished instead. Read this myth to discover what the power of such a strong friendship can bring.

VOCABULARY WORDS

tyrant (tī´ rənt) a ruler who holds complete power
❖ Someone who rules as a *tyrant* rarely wants to hear the opinions of others.

usurped (yo͞o zʉrpt´) took and held power, property, or a position by force and without rights
❖ The lords *usurped* the peasants' land.

philosopher (fə läs´ə fər) a person who studies the principles underlying conduct, thought, knowledge, and the nature of the universe
❖ A *philosopher* is often concerned with problems that affect society.

treason (trē´zən) an act of betrayal of one's country
❖ Benedict Arnold committed *treason* against the United States when he sold government secrets to the enemy.

penalty (pen´əl·tē) a punishment
❖ When Marla turned in her assignment late, her teacher deducted five points as a *penalty*.

stead (sted) the place or position of another
❖ The actor asked his daughter to attend the awards ceremony in his *stead*.

revoked (ri·vōkt´) canceled; called off
❖ The principal *revoked* the student's detention.

rebuked (ri·byo͞okt´) blamed; scolded
❖ She *rebuked* her son for raising his voice.

 **A**lthough Dionysius was known as the Tyrant of Syracuse—a name applied in ancient Greece to any absolute ruler who had usurped his power—he was not really cruel or cold-hearted. However, he was easily offended, and when he was annoyed he lost his temper and was much too severe with those who had offended him.

Pythias, a young scholar, had displeased the ruler because of his public speeches. When, together with his friend Damon, he was brought before Dionysius, he did not bow low as the king's subjects were in the habit of doing but stood facing the monarch with head held high.

"Don't you know you are supposed to bend the knee and ask my pardon for what you have done?" said Dionysius.

"I've done nothing of which I'm ashamed," said Pythias. "My school teaches that all men are equal and that no man should have absolute power over any other man."

"What school is that which holds such views?" asked Dionysius, beginning to lose his temper.

"The school of the philosopher Pythagoras," replied Pythias.

"It is treason to spread such a philosophy. It has been reported you say that kings have too much power, that their acts can be unwise and their laws unjust."

"That is true. It is also true that I am not afraid of being punished," said Pythias. "My school teaches patience."

"Your school!" said Dionysius angrily. "Very well, we shall put it to the test. We shall see how patient you can be. You will be imprisoned, and you will be given exactly one month to change your views. If you are still stubborn at the end of that time you will be sentenced to die. Have you anything more to say?"

"I have a request. Permit me to go to my home, put my affairs in order, and make arrangements for my mother and father."

Dionysius laughed scornfully. "Do you take me for a fool! Once I let you leave Syracuse, you will never return."

"I will guarantee my return," said Pythias.

"What sort of guarantee can you possibly give?" asked Dionysius.

Damon, who up to that moment had stood by silently, spoke.

"O king," he said. "I will be his guarantee. Pythias and I have been best friends since our boyhood. We are members of the same school. Let me take his place in prison. I know Pythias will never break a promise."

Dionysius was startled. "That is all very fine," he said. "But any man who takes the place of a prisoner is subject to the same penalty as the prisoner himself. Suppose that, in spite of your confidence, your friend fails to return and he receives the sentence of death—what then?"

"Then," said Damon calmly, "I will die in his stead."

"Well and good," said Dionysius to Damon. "I will accept the offer. But I warn you, if your friend doesn't return within a month from today, your life will not be spared. Now," he said, turning to the guards, "take him away."

Damon was imprisoned in a sunken chasm, one of those open caverns in the rocks peculiar to Syracuse. The most famous one was—and still is—called the Ear of Dionysius because the amazing acoustics made it possible for the Tyrant, standing above, to catch any plotting, even the faintest whisper, among the prisoners below. Dionysius went often to the Ear, but if he expected that Damon would fret or weep or cry for mercy, he was much mistaken. Never a word of complaint came from his sunken prison.

Two weeks went by, yet Damon showed no signs of worry. Some of his fellow prisoners mocked him for his folly; others sympathized with him. But Damon remained confident.

"He has been delayed—he has had trouble on the road or he has met with an accident. But I have faith in my friend. He will be here in time; there is nothing to fear."

Another two weeks passed and there was still no sign of Pythias. On the last day, Damon was brought out of his cell. His hands were bound and he was taken to the place of execution.

"What have you to say now?" sneered Dionysius. "Do you still believe in the noble words of your friend?"

"I believe what he believes," answered Damon. "And I believe in him."

As if in proof of these words, Pythias suddenly rushed in. His clothes were torn, his face was haggard, he could scarcely hold himself erect.

"Thank the gods I am here," he gasped. "Everything has been against me. My ship was wrecked on the way out, and later I was captured by robbers. But I did not lose my faith—and fate brought me back in time. Let me receive the sentence."

"The sentence of death is revoked," said Dionysius. "Neither of you shall die. Never have I witnessed such faith, such trust and loyalty. I am rebuked. I would exchange all my ministers and counselors for one such man as either Damon or Pythias."

Then, after a pause, he said, "Let me, in turn, ask a favor."

"What kind of favor?" inquired the two friends.

"Let me be the third in this friendship," said Dionysius.

READING FOR UNDERSTANDING

1. What has Pythias learned at his school?

2. Why does Dionysius imprison Pythias?

3. What will happen to Damon if Pythias does not return to Syracuse?

4. Why is Pythias late in returning to Syracuse?

5. What does Dionysius ask of Damon and Pythias at the end of the legend?

RESPONDING TO THE STORY

Damon and Pythias are such good friends that they are willing to risk their lives for each other. How do you feel about trust? Explain.

REVIEWING VOCABULARY

Fill in each blank with the correct word from the following list: *rebuked, treason, usurped, revoked, stead.*

1. Selling government secrets to an enemy is an act of

_____ .

2. Because I have stage fright, Corey offered to make the announcement in my _____ .

3. The principal _____ the children for having a food fight in the cafeteria.

4. My parents _____ my driving privileges when I missed my curfew.

5. The dictator's power was _____ by the leader of the revolution.

THINKING CRITICALLY

1. Why do you think Damon was so sure Pythias would return in time to save him?

2. Dionysius declares that Pythias will die if he does not change his views. The ruler comes very close to killing Damon in Pythias's place. Yet, at the end of the story, Dionysius wants to be friends with both young men. What brings about his change of heart?

WRITING PROJECTS

1. Write a scene for the story describing how Damon and Pythias might respond to Dionysius's request for their friendship.

2. Imagine that you are Damon. It is the day before you (or Pythias) will be put to death. Write a journal entry explaining your thoughts about Pythias's tardiness in returning to Syracuse.

THANK YOU M'AM

by Langston Hughes

People who are confused or in trouble show their emotions in different ways. Often, it is only with an effort that someone else can recognize what the problem behind the confusion and trouble really is. It takes a very special person to make that effort and to find a way to help.

Meet Mrs. Luella Bates Washington Jones, the heroine of the story. When a teenage boy tries to steal her purse, she reacts in an unexpected way. She understands that the boy needs her help, and she chooses a unique way of giving it to him. Read the story to find out what she does.

VOCABULARY WORDS

snatch (snach) to steal; to take

❖ Thieves tried to *snatch* Jaime's wallet from his backpack.

latching (lach´ing) grabbing; holding

❖ The small child was *latching* onto her mother's shirt.

barren (bar´ən) deserted; empty

❖ The house that was for sale looked *barren*.

stoop (sto͞op) a small porch at the door of a house

❖ The boy watched the people in the street from his *stoop*.

She was a large woman with a large purse that had everything in it but a hammer and nails. It had a long strap, and she carried it slung across her shoulder. It was about eleven o'clock at night, dark, and she was walking alone, when a boy ran up behind her and tried to snatch her purse. The strap broke with the sudden single tug the boy gave it from behind. But the boy's weight and the weight of the purse combined caused him to lose his balance. Instead of taking off full blast as he had hoped, the boy fell on his back on the sidewalk and his legs flew up. The large woman simply turned around and kicked him right square in his blue-jeaned sitter. Then she reached down, picked the boy up by his shirt front, and shook him until his teeth rattled.

After that the woman said, "Pick up my pocketbook, boy, and give it here."

She still held him tightly. But she bent down enough to permit him to stoop and pick up her purse. Then she said, "Now ain't you ashamed of yourself?"

Firmly gripped by his shirt front, the boy said, "Yes'm."

The woman said, "What did you want to do it for?"

The boy said, "I didn't aim to."

She said, "You a lie!"

By that time two or three people passed, stopped, turned to look, and some stood watching.

"If I turn you loose, will you run?" asked the woman.

"Yes'm," said the boy.

"Then I won't turn you loose," said the woman. She did not release him.

"Lady, I'm sorry," whispered the boy.

"Um-hum! Your face is dirty. I got a great mind to wash your face for you. Ain't you got nobody home to tell you to wash your face?"

"No'm," said the boy.

"Then it will get washed this evening," said the large woman, starting up the street, dragging the frightened boy behind her.

He looked as if he were fourteen or fifteen, frail and willow-wild, in tennis shoes and blue jeans.

The woman said, "You ought to be my son. I would teach you right from wrong. Least I can do right now is to wash your face. Are you hungry?"

"No'm," said the being-dragged boy. "I just want you to turn me loose."

"Was I bothering *you* when I turned that corner?" asked the woman.

"No'm."

"But you put yourself in contact with *me*," said the woman. "If you think that that contact is not going to last awhile, you got another thought coming. When I get through with you, sir, you are going to remember Mrs. Luella Bates Washington Jones."

Sweat popped out on the boy's face, and he began to struggle. Mrs. Jones stopped, jerked him around in front of her, put a half-nelson about his neck, and continued to drag him up the street. When she got to her door, she dragged the boy inside, down a hall, and into a large kitchenette-furnished room at the rear of the house. She switched on the light and left the door open. The boy could hear other roomers laughing and talking in the large house. Some of their doors were open, too, so he knew he and the woman were not alone. The woman still had him by the neck in the middle of her room.

She said, "What is your name?"

"Roger," answered the boy.

"Then, Roger, you go to that sink and wash your face," said the woman, whereupon she turned him loose—at last. Roger looked at the door—looked at the woman—looked at the door—*and went to the sink.*

"Let the water run until it gets warm," she said. "Here's a clean towel."

"You gonna take me to jail?" asked the boy, bending over the sink.

"Not with that face, I would not take you nowhere," said the woman. "Here I am trying to get home to cook me a bite to eat, and you snatch my pocketbook! Maybe you ain't been to your supper either, late as it be. Have you?"

"There's nobody home at my house," said the boy.

"Then we'll eat," said the woman. "I believe you're hungry—or been hungry—to try to snatch my pocketbook!"

"I want a pair of blue suede shoes," said the boy.

"Well, you didn't have to snatch *my* pocketbook to get some suede shoes," said Mrs. Luella Bates Washington Jones. "You could of asked me."

"M'am?"

The water dripping from his face, the boy looked at her. There was a long pause. A very long pause. After he had dried his face and not knowing what else to do, dried it again, the boy turned around, wondering what next. The door was open. He could make a dash for it down the hall. He could run, run, run, *run!*

The woman was sitting on the day bed. After a while she said, "I were young once and I wanted things I could not get."

There was another long pause. The boy's mouth opened. Then he frowned, not knowing he frowned.

The woman said, "Um-hum! You thought I was going to say *but,* didn't you? You thought I was going to say, *but I didn't snatch people's pocketbooks.* Well, I wasn't going to say that." Pause. Silence. "I have done things, too, which I would not tell you, son—neither tell God, if He didn't already know. Everybody's got something in common. So you set down while I fix us something to eat. You might run that comb through your hair so you will look presentable."

In another corner of the room behind a screen was a gas plate and an icebox. Mrs. Jones got up and went behind the screen. The woman did not watch the boy to see if he was going to run now, nor did she watch her purse, which she left behind her on the day bed. But the boy took care to sit on the far side of the room, away from the purse, where he thought she could easily see him out of the corner of her eye if she wanted to. He did not trust the woman *not* to trust him. And he did not want to be mistrusted now.

"Do you need somebody to go to the store," asked the boy, "maybe to get some milk or something?"

"Don't believe I do," said the woman, "unless you just want sweet milk yourself. I was going to make cocoa out of this canned milk I got here."

"That will be fine," said the boy.

She heated some lima beans and ham she had in the icebox, made the cocoa, and set the table. The woman did not ask the boy anything about where he lived, or his folks, or anything else that would embarrass him. Instead, as they ate, she told him about her job in a hotel beauty shop that stayed open late, what the work was like, and how all kinds of women came in and out, blondes, redheads, and Spanish. Then she cut him a half of her ten-cent cake.

"Eat some more, son," she said.

When they were finished eating, she got up and said, "Now here, take this ten dollars and buy yourself some blue suede shoes. And next time, do not make the mistake of latching onto *my* pocketbook *nor nobody else's*—because shoes got by devilish ways will burn your feet. I got to get my rest now. But from here on in, son, I hope you will behave yourself."

She led him down the hall to the front door and opened it. "Good night! Behave yourself, boy!" she said, looking out into the street as he went down the steps.

The boy wanted to say something other than, "Thank you, m'am," to Mrs. Luella Bates Washington Jones, but although his lips moved, he couldn't even say that as he turned at the foot of the barren stoop and looked up at the large woman in the door. Then she shut the door.

READING FOR UNDERSTANDING

1. What prevents the boy from running after he snatches the woman's purse?

2. Why does the woman take the boy to her home?

3. How does Mrs. Jones react when the boy tells her he tried to steal her pocketbook so he could buy a pair of blue suede shoes?

4. Why doesn't the boy run away while Mrs. Jones is cooking?

5. What does the boy say to Mrs. Jones after she gives him the ten dollars?

RESPONDING TO THE STORY

Sometimes simple acts of kindness can make a person change his or her way of life. If you were the boy in the story, do you think that you would stop stealing after having met Mrs. Jones? Explain your answer.

REVIEWING VOCABULARY

Match each word on the left with the correct definition on the right.

1. snatch   **a.** grabbing; getting hold of

2. latching   **b.** to steal; to take

3. barren   **c.** a small porch at the front of a house

4. stoop   **d.** deserted; empty

THINKING CRITICALLY

1. At one point in the story, the narrator says of the boy: "He could make a dash for it down the hall. He could run, run, run, *run!*" But just a few moments later the boy chooses to sit where Mrs. Jones can see him because he "did not want to be mistrusted now." Why do you think the boy undergoes this change?

2. Why do you think Mrs. Jones wants to help the boy?

WRITING PROJECTS

1. Imagine that you are Mrs. Jones. It is the day after the boy tried to steal your purse, and you are telling your friends at work about the events. In a paragraph, describe the boy and his actions.

2. Imagine that you are the boy, Roger. Days have gone by since you met Mrs. Jones, and you are sorry that you did not say anything when you left her home. Write a letter to her explaining your behavior.

THE MAGIC BOAT
retold by Moritz Jagendorf

What would you do if you saw a person or animal in distress? Would you go out of your way to help? Most people help others because they have compassion. Compassion is feeling sorrow or pity for another who is suffering or in trouble, accompanied by an urge to help.

While walking home one day, Wang sees an old man who has fallen into the river. Wang leaps into the rushing water to save the man. The man gives him a gift as an expression of his thanks. Little does Wang know that the old man's gift will completely change his future.

VOCABULARY WORDS

token (tō′kən) a sign or symbol
❖ She gave him the ring as a *token* of her affection.

frantic (frant′ik) desperate; frenzied
❖ The mother made a *frantic* search for her lost child.

minister (min′is·tər) a person who holds an important position in government
❖ The *minister* of health announced a new immunization program.

proclamation (präk′lə·mā′shən) a public announcement
❖ By *proclamation* of the king, the sixth of May will be a holiday.

worthy (wʉr′thē) being good enough; having enough value
❖ The paper was *worthy* of a perfect grade.

wily (wīl′ē) sly; crafty
❖ The fox is often a *wily* character in fables.

chaff (chaf) the inedible husks of a grain separated during threshing
❖ The peasants separated the wheat from the *chaff* using large wire mesh strainers.

misdeeds (mis·dēdz′) wrong actions; crimes
❖ His parents took away his allowance because of his *misdeeds*.

 **H**an folk, like folk everywhere in the world, after the day's hard work and their simple meal, sit around and talk. They talk of this and that and often they tell tales of what happened in the good old days.

In those good old days there lived a woodcutter named Wang. He was a good man and worked hard to support himself and his old mother.

One day, as he was walking home from work in the hills, a load of dry branches on his back, he came to a wide river over which there was a narrow wooden bridge for crossing. As he got near the bridge he saw an old man on it. The old man had just reached the middle when a gust of wind flung him to the side. He lost his balance and fell into the wildly rushing water below and began battling to reach the bank. But he was not strong enough.

Wang threw down his backpack and leaped into the river. He was strong and with a few strokes reached the struggling old man and, holding him, swam to the bank. The old man was half frozen and trembling from the cold, so Wang put him on his back and took him to the old man's home. The man thanked Wang again and again for having saved his life.

After they dried themselves and rested a while, the old man took out a little wooden box from under his bed and said, "I thank you for your help and good heart. Such kindness should be well rewarded." He slid open the top of the box and drew out a little paper boat. "See this little boat. I shall give it to you as a token of my gratitude."

Wang looked at the paper boat. It was complete in every way, with a covered bunk for sleeping, oars, rudder, and anchor.

"Dear friend," the old man said, "this is not a child's toy; it is a magic boat that will save your life as you saved mine. Take it, and take good care of it."

Wang took the boat as the old man continued, "Soon a great flooding rain will come here, and your paper boat will turn into a great wooden boat where you will be safe. You can take as many animals as you wish, but do not take any man on it. If you do, it will bring you harm."

The old man again thanked Wang; then they bade each other goodbye.

Holding the boat carefully, the woodcutter picked up his load of wood and started home. No sooner did he reach there than it began to rain. Thunder shook his walls and lightning flashed all around. It rained for many days without stopping. The water rose to the threshold of Wang's house. Wang and his mother were frantic. Then he suddenly remembered the paper boat in the wooden box, which he had hidden in a crack in the wall. He took out the box and put the boat on the water. It immediately turned into wood and began to grow bigger and bigger. In a short time it was a full-size river-going boat. Wang and his mother got in. The wind swished the rain in all directions. Animals appeared everywhere, struggling in the water: snakes, animals with fur, even bees and ants. They all swam around the boat and Wang and his mother took them up as fast as they could.

Suddenly Wang heard someone shouting, "Wang! Wang! Help! Save me!"

Wang looked and there was Chang, the son of one of the rich men in the village. Wang forgot the warning of the old man and stretched out an oar and helped Chang get onto the boat.

The rain continued for a long time. Then it stopped and the boat touched dry land. Everyone was glad to leave.

When they were gone, the boat began shrinking and

again became a paper boat, which Wang put back into the little box for safekeeping.

Chang looked in astonishment at the change. Then he spoke, "Truly this is a magic boat! Where did you get it, Wang?"

"An old man whom I saved from drowning gave it to me."

"You are a lucky man, Wang, to have such a wonderful magic boat. Why not give it to the Emperor? He would surely reward you richly for such a marvelous gift."

"I cannot go to the capital to see the Emperor! I must stay here and work to support my old mother."

"Let me go with the boat instead and I will tell the Emperor that you sent it to him. Then I will come back and tell you what reward he has given to you. Maybe you will be made minister and live with your mother in a mansion."

"Go, good friend Chang. I will wait here for the glad news," said Wang.

So Chang went to the palace with the little box. He told the palace guards his mission and was taken to the throne room.

"Your Majesty," Chang said, "I have brought you a wonderful magic paper boat that turns into a real boat when you float it in the water." But he never said one word about Wang.

The Emperor was pleased and appointed Chang to a high office and gave him a mansion in which to live. There Chang stayed, forgetting all about Wang.

Days went by and Wang waited in his hut for Chang. He kept on cutting wood and selling it to support himself and his mother.

Often he wondered why Chang did not come back as he had promised and he wondered what had happened to his magic boat.

One day he decided to go to the capital to find out. After arranging for someone to take care of his old mother he set out, carrying some clothes and bedding in bundles on both ends of a slender pole. When he reached the capital he found lodging in an inn. The innkeeper told him that Chang passed by the street every morning on his way to the Emperor's court. The next day Wang waited on the street. Soon he saw Chang coming in his sedan chair, preceded by attendants carrying banners and musicians playing gongs and drums.

Wang shouted greetings to him. Chang was shocked when he saw Wang. He was frightened that Wang had come to claim his position and wealth. So he ordered the guards to drive Wang away and not spare the use of their sticks. This they did readily, cutting Wang's face and beating all his body.

Wang limped away as best he could and lay down by the wayside, unable to walk. Then a wonderful thing happened. Some of the animals he had saved from drowning were nearby and recognized him.

A snake lying not far off sidled up to him as he lay there groaning. It was a snake with magic powers, as many animals had in those olden days. He began licking the cuts on Wang's face. At once he felt no more pain.

Then the snake glided swiftly away and returned with a few magic healing plants in his mouth. He touched Wang's wounds with the plants and the wounds closed at once. Even the pain where he had been hit on his shoulders and legs was gone.

He rested for a time and then decided to find out why his friend had acted so meanly. As he rose, the snake said to him, "Take some of the miracle healing plants with you. You may need them someday."

Wang thanked the snake and started for the palace. When he came near the gate, he saw a crowd gathered around a proclamation on the wall, reading it. The large Chinese characters told them that the Emperor's daughter suddenly had become very ill, and the ruler promised no end of riches and even the Princess in marriage to the man who would cure her.

At once Wang thought of the miracle-curing plants the snake had given him and he asked to be taken to see the sick Princess. Soon he was in the chamber where she was lying in a curtained bed. The Emperor was there also, watching to see what Wang would do.

Wang took a miracle plant and gave it to a trusted lady-in-waiting. She rubbed the Princess from head to toe with it. At once color came back to her cheeks and lips. The lady-in-waiting kept on rubbing her with the miracle plant and soon after Wang left the Princess's room, she got up and seemed all well.

Then the Emperor said, "You are a wonderful doctor, Wang, and I want you to stay in my palace. If my daughter desires it, you may marry her."

When Chang saw what had happened, he was frightened lest his treachery be discovered.

He went to the Emperor. "Your Majesty," he said, "you will let an ignorant man marry your daughter because he has a magic healing plant any other man could also have found. Why not first put him to tests to see if he is worthy of marrying a princess?"

The Emperor thought this was good advice, so he said to Chang, "You think of the proper tests to try his worthiness."

This was just what the wily fellow wanted. He went at once to the Chief Advisor of the palace, who was his friend.

"I bring you a bar of gold, dear friend, for the many favors you have done for me. Now, once again, I will ask you to do something for me. You know the Emperor will let that peasant woodcutter marry his daughter. She is worthy of a better man, and the good Emperor has agreed to the advice I have given him. I told him to put Wang to some tests to prove himself more than a peasant. Help me to think of some tasks in which he is sure to fail, for Wang is no friend of mine."

"Nor of mine," said the advisor. "I know of one task that neither Wang nor any other man can do."

"What is it, good friend?"

"Take two measures of chaff and mix them together with two measures of fine sesame seeds and then order him to separate one from the other by the time the sun reaches the center of the sky. No man can do that, and surely not a common woodcutter."

Chang was pleased and returned to the Emperor and told him of the test to be set to Wang to prove himself worthy of a princess. The Emperor agreed and ordered that chaff and sesame seeds be mixed and set in the garden pavilion. Then Wang was called.

"Wang," said the Emperor, "You are an unknown woodcutter. Before I will let you marry my daughter, you must show yourself worthy of her. Here on this bench is a chest in which two *tou* of chaff and two *tou* of sesame seeds are mixed. You must separate the sesame seeds from the chaff by the time the sun is in the middle of Heaven. That will prove you are more than just a woodcutter."

The Emperor left and Wang was alone with the sesame seeds and the chaff. No—he was not alone. In the garden insects and ants all around him were busy with their daily chores.

Now it so happened that among the ants were some who were on the magic boat with Wang. They saw how downhearted he looked.

"Why so sad?" the ants asked.

"I am sad because I was told I would have to separate the sesame seeds from the chaff by the time the sun is in the center of Heaven. No man can do that."

"True," the ants said, and they shook their jointed bodies with laughter. "True, no man can do it, but ants can. You saved our lives, and now we will help you. Just watch us."

By this time hundreds of ants had gathered around Wang.

"Come to work," shouted the ants who had spoken to Wang.

The ants set to work at once, falling over one another, pushing, jostling, busily separating the sesame seeds from the chaff, and, before you could count to ten, the work was done, and the sun was not yet in the middle of Heaven.

The sun moved slowly in its path and soon was at the very middle when Chang and the Chief Advisor burst into the pavilion, the Emperor following slowly. They all stopped in amazement when they saw the seeds and the chaff carefully separated into two heaps. Not a single one was intermixed with the other.

"That is truly wonderful," said the Emperor.

"But not wonderful enough for a common woodcutter to marry a princess, Your Majesty," said the Chief Advisor. "Put him to one more test, which will be the last. If he succeeds, he will be truly worthy, Your Majesty. Here is the supreme test I would suggest. Seat the Princess among fifty-three maidens, all dressed alike, all sitting in flower chairs. If he can choose the Princess from among the fifty-four, then he can marry her."

The Emperor agreed, and the trial was set for the next day. It would be held again in the royal garden.

Wang could not sleep from excitement and worry. When the first glow of dawn came into the sky, he was in the garden looking at the fifty-four "flower chairs" set out.

The garden was full of morning life:—ants, insects, birds, butterflies, and pigeons were busy hunting, and bees were zooming from flower to flower in their usual way. Some of those who had been sheltered by Wang recognized him.

"Why so sad, Master Wang?" they zoomed. "Why so sad when all around you is sunshine and warmth?"

"I am sad because soon I will be given a test that I know I will fail."

"What is that terrible test?" they zoomed merrily.

"To find which is the Princess among fifty-four maidens, all dressed alike and seated in these flower chairs you see there. How can I find her among fifty-four?"

"Easily, easily," zoomed the bees. "Easily, with our help. You helped us, now we will help you. The Princess loves bees and sweet honey. We will swarm around her flower chair. In this way you will be able to recognize her."

A door opened, and the maidens, chattering, laughing, all dressed alike, seated themselves in the flower chairs. The chairs were then borne on the shoulders of chair carriers in a procession around the garden. Chang, the Chief Advisor, and the Emperor also came out. Wang looked at the girls, who smiled and blushed.

"Look slowly and carefully," said the Emperor, who had begun to like Wang.

Wang looked carefully from one maiden to another. Then he came to the maiden seated in the chair around which bees were zooming merrily, as they had promised.

"That is the Princess," Wang said, as he pointed to the maiden around whom the bees were swarming merrily.

"That is the Princess," Wang shouted a second time.

"Truly," said the Emperor, "Wang, you are worthy of marrying my daughter."

And married they were and lived a happy life, and so did Wang's mother.

As for Chang, when the Emperor heard the complete story, Chang was punished properly for his misdeeds.

READING FOR UNDERSTANDING

1. How does the magic boat come into Wang's possession?

2. How does Wang use the magic boat to help others?

3. What does Chang do with the magic boat?

4. How is Wang able to cure the Princess?

5. Why does the Emperor test Wang?

RESPONDING TO THE STORY

Wang cares about and helps others who are in trouble. What are some everyday activities that you can do to help others in need?

REVIEWING VOCABULARY

1. Robert's *misdeeds*, which included robbery and assault, led him to a life **(a)** that others admired **(b)** in prison **(c)** in the country.

2. Daniel gave me a photo of himself as a *token* of our friendship so I would always **(a)** ignore him **(b)** remember him **(c)** call him.

3. When Sharon heard that a hurricane was coming, she became *frantic*, or **(a)** full of hope **(b)** calm and collected **(c)** full of panic.

4. Vice president and prime *minister* are both titles of important **(a)** history books **(b)** factory workers **(c)** government officials.

5. Emily was *worthy* of winning the prize because her performance was **(a)** great **(b)** average **(c)** boring.

THINKING CRITICALLY

1. Suppose the Emperor had given Wang the choice of whether or not to punish Chang. What do you think Wang would have done?

2. Do you think that even if Wang had remembered the old man's warning he would have refused to help Chang during the flood? Why or why not?

WRITING PROJECTS

1. Write a paragraph describing another test that Wang must pass in order to marry the Princess.

2. Write a newspaper article about Wang's deeds. Include the comments and reactions of people who might have witnessed one of the events in the story.

A PRESENT FOR GRANDFATHER

by Jusran Safano

Have you ever heard the expression, "It's better to give than to receive"? Many people get a great deal of satisfaction from sharing with others. The joy of giving comes from knowing that you were responsible for making someone else happy.

Bakri wants to help his sick grandfather feel better. He decides to look for muncang nuts, which his grandfather particularly enjoys, to give him. Yet he finds himself in an uncomfortable situation when some of his friends arrive, also wanting to gather the nuts. In the tale you are about to read, you will discover the unique way in which Bakri and his friends resolve the situation.

VOCABULARY WORDS

mosque (mäsk) a Moslem house of worship
❖ Many people in Egypt go to a *mosque* to pray.

summoning (sum´ən ing) calling
❖ My mother was *summoning* us to dinner with a whistle.

diligent (dil´ə jənt) careful and persistent
❖ The judges were impressed with the *diligent* effort Barbara made on her project.

wholeheartedly (hōl´härt´id lē) with great enthusiasm; sincerely
❖ All the members of the club support that candidate *wholeheartedly*.

sarong (sə rông´) a bright-colored skirt worn by men and women in Southeast Asia and the Pacific islands
❖ She wore a *sarong* while visiting her relatives in Malaysia.

unison (yōōn´ə sən) in harmony
❖ The school chorus sang in *unison*.

sheepishly (shēp´ish lē) with embarrassment; with shy awkwardness
❖ The boy *sheepishly* told his parents that he had broken the new vase.

bound (bound) headed toward
❖ The soldiers were *bound* for the battlefield.

There was a young boy named Bakri who lived in a lovely village far in the mountains. It was a lonely village, yes, but also very quiet and peaceful. A swift-flowing stream tumbled down from the mountains and ran through the village. The villagers could hear the rush of its crystal-clear waters as they lay in their beds at night. And then at dawn every morning they could hear another sound that also formed part of their way of life. This was the beating of a big drum in the mosque that stood across the river, and then the echoing voice from the mosque tower summoning them to morning prayers.

It was Bakri's grandfather who sang out this call to the village every morning. He had a strong, powerful voice that seemed to fill the heavens, and he was very diligent about his duties, never missing a single morning. But on this particular morning there was no sound of his voice calling from the mosque.

Bakri thought this was very strange and began worrying about what might have happened. Was Grandfather sick or something? At first Bakri thought he should go to his grandfather's house to see what was the matter instead of going to the mosque to pray. But somehow he didn't want to start the day without going to prayers at dawn. And maybe someone at the mosque might know what had happened to his grandfather.

At the mosque he looked everywhere for the old man, but there was no trace of him, and nobody knew where he was. Is he sick at home? wondered the boy. When the prayers began, Bakri tried to calm his thoughts and put everything out of his mind so he could pray wholeheartedly, but still he kept worrying.

After prayers, he started for his grandfather's place, but then he stopped to think. Shouldn't he take a present to Grandfather? And wasn't this just the time of year for gathering the muncang, a kind of nut that his grandfather found most delicious? Yes, first he'd go gather nuts for Grandfather.

So away he went hurrying through the mists of early morning, making his way toward Nut Hill, where the finest muncangs grew. It was cold, but he had worn a warm sarong to the mosque, and now he pulled this closely about him as he made his way into the mountains.

As he went along, he thought what a pleasant surprise it would be for Grandfather if he could gather many nuts at Nut Hill. The shells were very, very hard, and after he'd eaten the nuts from inside, then Grandfather could use the shells for carving the lovely finger rings that he could make so well. Why, his grandfather's rings were famous in many villages, and it would be easy to sell them for even fifty rupiahs each. And if he could gather enough nuts for a hundred rings, just think how much money Grandfather could make. Surely he'd be so happy that he wouldn't be sick any more. Let's see, Bakri said to himself, if I multiply fifty rupiahs times one hundred rings, how much money is that? He tried counting it all out on his fingers, but somehow he couldn't get the answer. He was just in the third grade at school, you see. But, anyway, Grandfather was sure to be pleased.

Bakri began whistling a happy tune, but then, suddenly, he stopped. Suppose some of the other boys from the village had beat him to Nut Hill and already gathered all the nuts that had fallen to the ground overnight? And he hurried faster and faster.

He arrived at the foot of Nut Hill just as the sun rose over the horizon, painting the sky a beautiful red. He ran and ran, up and up, frightening the flying foxes that were on their way back to their nests to sleep through the day. Reaching the top of the hill, he stopped for breath. He was delighted to see that he was the first boy there; there wasn't a sign of the others yet.

In the grove of muncang trees, the ground was covered with nuts. There'd been a strong wind the night before, which had knocked down more nuts than usual. Singing merrily to himself, Bakri began gathering the nuts. He used his sarong to make a bag for holding the nuts. It was his best sarong, but he told himself that he'd wash it carefully when he got home.

Suddenly he heard some voices. Someone was coming up the hill. It must be the other boys from the village, he told himself. And if they find that I came here so early, without even asking them to come with me, and that I've already gathered all the fallen nuts—well, they'll be angry and probably take all the nuts away from me. Why, I'll be lucky if they don't beat me up as well for being so greedy.

His only chance was to hide before the other boys saw him. Running over to one side of the grove, he crawled inside a clump of bushes and hid himself as best he could.

He sat there in the bushes, praying they wouldn't see him. He kept so still that he almost stopped breathing. Soon he saw five boys come over the crest of the hill. All of them were bigger than he.

The boys stopped at the edge of the grove and looked around at the ground, puzzled. "We've come too late," one of them cried in disappointment.

"There's not a single nut left on the ground," another said.

"What bad luck!" said a third. "And after coming all this way."

"Someone got here much earlier," said the tallest boy.

Almost in unison all the boys cried out: "Bakri! That's who must have been here." And one added: "He's always up before dawn anyway to go to the mosque."

Hearing all this from his hiding place in the bushes, Bakri became more and more frightened and prayed all the harder.

"Look!" one of the boys said, pointing to a moist patch of dew under a tree. "Here's his footprints still showing. He must have just left here carrying the nuts with him."

"Quick," said another, "if we hurry, we can catch him and take the nuts away from him."

The oldest boy was staring thoughtfully at the ground. Finally he said: "No, that wouldn't be fair. After all, didn't he get up early enough to go to the mosque and still get here before us, while we were snugly sleeping in our beds? Well, then, I say he deserves the nuts, and we deserve nothing. If we want nuts, we'd better get up early instead of taking his nuts away from him. And we'd better start going to the mosque at dawn too."

The other boys looked at him sheepishly. They knew, of course, that he was right. If they hadn't been so lazy, they'd have had nuts of their own. Not saying anything to each other, they started back, walking slowly down the hill.

Watching from the bushes, Bakri was deeply moved. He was thankful that his prayers had been answered and the boys hadn't seen him, and he was also filled with pity by the sad looks on the boys' faces. Suddenly he stood up, gave a loud yell, and went running after the boys.

The boys stopped and turned toward Bakri. They were astonished to see him running toward them.

When he reached them, Bakri said: "I'm sorry I took all the nuts. Here, you take part of them. After all, we're all good friends and should share and share alike."

The five stood there, looking first at Bakri and then at each other. Finally the tallest said: "No, no thank you, Bakri. They're all your nuts because you got up early and came and gathered them."

"Don't be silly," answered Bakri, grabbing the boy's hand. "I really want you to have them. I was going to take them to my grandfather because he didn't give the call to prayers this morning and I thought he might be ill. But he'll be just as happy with only my share."

"Yes," said one of the boys, "I saw him talking to a neighbor this morning and heard him say he's caught a bad cold but that he'll be able to go to the mosque again in a few days."

"That's what we'll do, then," said the tallest boy. "Bakri will share his nuts with us, and then we'll all go and give all of them to Bakri's grandfather. Then he'll get well and strong again in a hurry, and once more we can hear his powerful voice rolling out over the village as it calls us to prayers."

So that's how it was decided. The weather was fine and clear. The boys put their arms around each other's shoulders and walked on down the hill in the sunlight, singing happily, bound for the home of Bakri's grandfather.

READING FOR UNDERSTANDING

1. What two sounds do the villagers hear at dawn every morning?

2. After Bakri notices that his grandfather's voice has not summoned the villagers to prayers, why does he not go immediately to his grandfather's house?

3. Why does Bakri's grandfather like muncang nuts?

4. Why do the older boys guess that it was Bakri who gathered all the nuts before they came?

5. What solution do the boys arrive at for sharing the muncang nuts?

RESPONDING TO THE STORY

Bakri and his friends realize that sharing what they value makes everybody happy. Think about someone you have heard or read about who has had an effect on another person through the act of sharing. In a short paragraph, explain what happened.

REVIEWING VOCABULARY

Fill in each blank with the correct word from the following list: *wholeheartedly, diligent, unison, summoning, sheepishly.*

1. Miguel is hard-working and _____ when it comes to his studies.

2. The puppy looked at me _____ when I discovered the overturned garbage can.

3. The ballerinas moved as one dancer; every movement was in _____ .

4. Romeo and Juliet loved each other completely and _____ .

5. The lawyer is _____ everyone who witnessed the accident to appear in court.

THINKING CRITICALLY

1. Bakri and the tallest boy disagree about who should keep the nuts. Which one of the boys do you think makes the stronger argument? Explain your answer.

2. Why do you think the boys decide to share their nuts with Bakri's grandfather? What details in the story make you think so?

WRITING PROJECTS

1. Write a scene for the story showing what takes place when all the boys present their muncang nuts to Bakri's grandfather.

2. Imagine that you are one of the older boys. Write a letter to a friend from another village describing what took place on Nut Hill.

RICH MAN, POOR MAN
retold by Jane Yolen

Have you ever heard the saying "an eye for an eye, a tooth for a tooth"? It means that a person who hurts someone else should receive punishment equivalent to the injury suffered by the victim. This idea of fairness comes from a set of laws written almost 4,000 years ago. This idea also plays a very important part in the story you are about to read.

It is a time of great hunger in Africa. A poor man wants to find a way to make his humble meal of maize taste good. Unfortunately, his creative solution gets him into serious trouble. Only by convincing people to believe in "an eye for an eye" can a wise man get the poor man out of trouble.

VOCABULARY WORDS

famine (fam´in) a great shortage of food
❖ People died from hunger during the *famine*.

severe (sə·vir´) very serious
❖ Her stomachache was so *severe* that she went to a doctor.

scrounging (skrounj´ing) searching about for something that is needed and is not easily available
❖ He was *scrounging* in his pocket for a quarter.

maize (māz) corn
❖ Native Americans cultivated and ate *maize*.

bleats (blētz) makes sounds characteristic of a goat
❖ The goat *bleats* when it is hungry.

It happened one time, long, long ago, that in one of the villages of the Akamba, there were two men who lived as neighbors. One was rich, and the other was poor, but they were friends. The poor man worked for the rich man, helping him. Now a famine came to the land. And when the suffering became very severe, the rich man forgot the poor man, and the poor man who used to eat at his friend's house now had to beg from him. Finally, the rich man chased him away altogether, because a rich man cannot remain the friend of a poor person for too long, and he felt that even the scraps he now gave his poor neighbor were just too much.

One day, this poor man was scrounging about in the village for something to eat. He was given *maize* by a man who took pity on him, and he took it home to his wife, and she cooked it. But they had no meat with which to make it into soup, nor did they have salt with which to season it. So the man said, "I will go see if my rich friend is having a good soup tonight." He went and found that the meal cooking there gave out a nice sweet smell. So he returned back to his house, got the cooked *maize,* and brought it back to the rich man's house, where he sat against the wall and ate it, breathing in the smell that came from the rich man's meal. When he had eaten, he returned to his own home.

Another day, the poor man saw the rich man and went up to him and said, "I came a few days ago, while you were eating your food, and I sat by the wall, and ate my food together with the delicious smell that came from your food."

The rich man was furious, and he said, "So that's why my food was completely tasteless that day! It was you who ate the good taste from my food, and you must pay me for it! I'm taking you to the judge to file a case against you." And he did that, and the poor man was told to pay one goat to the rich man for eating the sweet smell from his food. But the poor man could not afford even one goat, and he broke down and cried as he went back to his house.

On his way home, he met a wise man and a speechmaker, and he told him what had happened. The wise man gave him a goat, and told him to keep that goat until he came back. Now, the judge had appointed a certain day when the poor man was to pay the rich man; and on that day, many people came together to witness the payment. The wise man came also, and when he saw the people talking, he asked, "Why are you making so much fuss here?" The judge said, "This poor man is supposed to pay this rich man a goat for the smell he breathed from the rich man's food." The wise man asked his first question again, and he was given the same answer. So the wise man said, "Will you let me give another judgment on this case?" The people said, "Yes, if you are a good judge!" So he went on to say, "A man who steals must give back only as much as he has taken, no more, no less."

When the people asked him how he could pay back just the smell of good food, the wise man replied, "I will show you!" Then he turned to the rich man, and said to him, "Rich man, I am going to hit this goat, and when it bleats, I want you to take its bleating sound! You are not to touch this poor man's goat, unless he touched your food." Then he said to the people, "Listen now, while I pay back the rich man." So he beat the goat, and it bleated, and he said to the rich man, "Take that sound as payment for the smell of your good food!"

READING FOR UNDERSTANDING

1. How does the rich man treat the poor man after the famine begins?

2. Why is the poor man not satisfied with his meal of *maize*?

3. Why does the rich man file a case against the poor man?

4. How does the poor man get the goat he needs to pay the rich man?

5. What does the wise man propose to the rich man as payment for the smell of his food?

RESPONDING TO THE STORY

The judge gave the poor man a more severe punishment than he deserved, but the wise man treated him fairly. Do you know or have you heard or read about someone who received an unfair punishment for something he or she did wrong? Describe the situation and tell how you think he or she could have been treated more fairly.

REVIEWING VOCABULARY

1. *Maize*, which has been used for thousands of years, is a type of **(a)** food **(b)** clothing **(c)** shelter.

2. A great *famine* swept through the land after many months of no **(a)** harvest **(b)** rain **(c)** snow.

3. The *bleats* of the goats filled the entire **(a)** neighborhood **(b)** barnyard **(c)** schoolyard.

4. The girl was *scrounging* for a scrap of paper because her notebook was **(a)** not available **(b)** at hand **(c)** closed.

5. His mother's *severe* look let him know that he had done something **(a)** good **(b)** kind **(c)** wrong.

THINKING CRITICALLY

1. Why do you think the rich man became so angry with the poor man?

2. Do you think that the poor man's payment was fair? Explain.

WRITING PROJECTS

1. Imagine you were in the courtroom during the poor man's trial. Write a transcript of what the lawyers for each side argued while trying to win the case.

2. Write a speech from the point of view of one of the villagers who came to witness the poor man's payment. Try to convince your fellow villagers to force the current judge to resign and make the wise man judge in his place.

THE DANCING KETTLE

retold by Yoshiko Uchida

*In order to achieve our goals and dreams, we often need
to work with others. Surprisingly, sometimes the people
from whom we least expect help turn out to be the most
helpful. These people may even end up doing more than
helping us. They may become our friends.*

*A junkman finds himself the happy owner of a dancing
teakettle. Instead of being frightened by the extraordinary
kettle, he promises to take good care of it. Soon the
junkman and the teakettle form a business partnership
and a friendship. Find out how two characters working
together can make their dreams come true.*

VOCABULARY WORDS

tatami (tə·tä´mē) a floor mat woven of rice straw, used in Japanese homes to sit on
❖ The family sat at a low table on a *tatami*.

hibachi (hē·bä´chē) a charcoal-burning grill of Japanese design
❖ The priest heated water for tea on a *hibachi*.

sprouted (sprout´id) grew
❖ The plant *sprouted* beautiful flowers.

pranced (pranst) moved about in a lively manner; danced about
❖ The excited child *pranced* about the room.

glee (glē) joy; extreme happiness
❖ She was filled with *glee* because her parents were coming home.

furoshiki (fyo͞o·rō·shē´kē) a piece of cloth, traditionally used in Japan for wrapping things
❖ The man wrapped the basket of plums in a brightly colored *furoshiki*.

High up in the wooded hills of Japan, there once lived a priest in a beautiful old temple. He was a good and kindly man and was known for his love of beautiful things. He liked especially to collect teacups and kettles, and used them often in performing the formal tea ceremony.

One day he discovered a particularly beautiful teakettle and brought it back to the temple with him.

"My, but it is lovely," he murmured as he stroked the smooth sides of the kettle. He placed it carefully on a small teakwood table, and sat back on a little cushion on the *tatami* to admire its shape and beauty.

As the old priest sat in the sunny little room looking at his precious new kettle, his head slowly began to nod . . . nod . . . nod. . . . Outside, the tall pine trees swayed in the breeze and whispered softly to the priest. Before long he was sound asleep.

Suddenly the kettle began to wiggle! Out popped a head on top. Then out came two arms, and finally two legs. With a ker-plunk it jumped right off the table and began to dance around the room.

Just then, two other priests of the temple happened to be walking by. They tapped on the old priest's door, but, hearing no answer, pushed the sliding doors open just a tiny bit. As they peered into the room what did they see but a kettle with arms and legs dancing around the sleeping priest!

"Wh-what is this? What has happened to the kettle?" shouted one of the priests.

"Get up, sir! Get up!" shouted the other to the old priest.

The old priest grunted and shook the sleep from his eyes.

"What is all this noise? What is the trouble, my friends?" he asked.

"Look at your kettle! It's walking! It's dancing! Why, it must be haunted!" they exclaimed.

The old priest rubbed his eyes and looked at the table, but now the kettle was back in place just as it had been before.

"Ho, ho, my young friends," laughed the priest. "What are you talking about? You must both be dreaming."

"But the kettle *was* dancing. We saw it with our own eyes," they answered as they stared at the shiny new kettle which now sat quietly on the table.

"Come, come, you interrupted my lovely afternoon nap," said the old priest, and he again closed his eyes.

The two young priests couldn't understand what had happened, and shaking their heads, they left the room.

That night the old priest filled his new kettle and decided to boil some water for tea. He placed it on the little *hibachi* in his room and sat down to wait for the water to boil. Suddenly the kettle shouted, "Help! This is hot!" Out came its legs and off it hopped onto the floor.

The old priest was so surprised he could scarcely believe his eyes. "Help! Help!" he called. "This kettle is alive!"

His friends quickly rushed to his room and caught the dancing, hopping kettle, but when they had it in their hands, it was just an ordinary teakettle. There were no arms or legs to be seen.

"What have I bought?" asked the old priest sadly. "Surely it must be an evil thing, for it is no ordinary teakettle. I will give it to the junkman tomorrow."

And so early the next morning the old priest gave his teakettle to the junkman.

"Why, this is a beautiful kettle," said the junkman. "I shall keep it for myself," and he carried it home, whistling a happy little tune.

That night as he sat admiring the kettle, it again sprouted a head and two arms and legs. It jumped off the table and began to dance around the surprised junkman.

"My goodness! What sort of creature are you anyway?" he asked.

"Why, I am a very, very special kind of a teakettle. If you take good care of me, I can be very useful to you, but you must not fill me with water and put me over a fire like other pots and pans. Do you think you can feed me once in a while and take good care of me?" asked the kettle.

"Of course, of course I can," answered the man. He was still so surprised, his eyes looked like two round balls. "Tell me more about yourself," he added.

"When I was in the temple I had a terrible time. They would not feed me, and the old priest filled me with water and put me over glowing coals. Oh, I shudder to think of it," sighed the kettle. "Now if you know how to care for me, I can bring you much good luck. Did you know that I can dance and sing and do all sorts of fancy tricks?"

"Did you say you can dance and sing and do tricks?" asked the junkman. "Why, we could start a little theater out in the streets. People would pay money to see a teakettle that can dance, and then I would be able to feed you well and take very good care of you too. What do you think of that?"

"A fine idea! A lovely idea! Here, I will dance for you right now," said the kettle, and with a clinkety-clank and a skippety-hop it pranced about the junkman as he sang and clapped his hands.

The kettle and the junkman worked together for many days and at last they were ready to open their little street theater. The junkman pasted signs and posters about the streets of the town, telling everyone to come to see the dancing kettle. Then at night he stood beside his little theater shouting, "Come one, come all! See a teakettle that can dance and sing! Come see a kettle that can do tricks!"

Soon the little children and their mothers and fathers, and sisters and brothers, and aunts and uncles, and grandmothers and grandfathers came streaming out to see the kettle dance and sing. The children laughed and clapped their hands in glee as the kettle danced about the little stage.

People from villages near and far came to see this strange teakettle, and one day the kettle decided it would do something even more wonderful than just dancing or singing. It crossed the stage of the little theater balanced on a tightrope strung high in the air. When the people saw this, they shouted and clapped their hands, and threw gold coins onto the stage. Soon so many people wanted to see the kettle that they crowded and squeezed and pushed, even for a tiny glimpse.

Each day the junkman fed the kettle well and took good care of it. Each night he counted the gold coins that the people threw, and slowly the shiny golden stacks grew higher and higher.

"My, we are fast becoming rich," he said to the kettle with a big smile. But the junkman was not a greedy person and when he had saved a little money he said to the kettle, "You must be growing tired of dancing and singing every day, and I certainly have all the money I want now. Wouldn't you like to stop dancing and spend a quiet and peaceful life?"

"Oh, yes, indeed I would," said the kettle. "You are a good and kind man, my friend."

And so they closed their little street theater and decided to live quietly and peacefully.

As the junkman thought about the success which the kettle had brought him, he suddenly remembered the old priest who had given it to him.

"Why, I must go to thank the priest," he thought. "And I have an excellent idea!" So one bright, sunny morning when the skies were blue and clear, he decided to set out on his visit. He carefully polished the teakettle and wrapped it in a gay, bright *furoshiki*. He then put on his very best clothes, put half of all the money he had earned into a leather pouch, and started up the wooded hillside to the temple.

When he arrived at the temple, the priest was surprised to see him.

"What brings you here, my friend?" asked the priest.

So the junkman told the priest all about his wonderful kettle and of the street theater which he had.

"And I have you to thank for all my success," he added, "for if you hadn't given me the kettle all this would never have happened. I have brought half of my earnings for the temple, and I shall return the kettle to you, for it is really yours. I know you will take good care of it, and I am sure it will be happier here in this beautiful temple where others may come to admire its beauty."

"You are a generous and good man, my friend," said the priest. "Surely you will be blessed with many happy days, and we shall always remember you here in the temple."

"Take good care of my friend, the teakettle, won't you?" called the junkman as he was leaving.

"Indeed we will," the priest called back, as he watched the junkman walk slowly into the pine trees and down the wooded slope.

And indeed he did take good care of the little teakettle. Never again did the old priest try to boil water in it. He placed it carefully on his beautiful teakwood table, where many people who had heard of the dancing kettle came to admire it. From that day on, the kettle had a very special place in the temple, and it lived happily and peacefully ever after.

READING FOR UNDERSTANDING

1. What explanation do the two young priests give for the kettle's dancing?

2. How does the junkman promise to take care of the kettle?

3. What happens during the kettle's most exciting performance?

4. Why does the junkman suggest that the kettle stop dancing for the street theater?

5. Why does the junkman return the kettle to the temple?

RESPONDING TO THE STORY

In this folktale, a junkman and a dancing teakettle work together to achieve their goals. In a short paragraph, describe a situation in which you and another person or group of people cooperated to bring about the goal all of you desired.

REVIEWING VOCABULARY

Match each word on the left with the correct definition on the right.

1. *tatami*   a. extreme happiness; joy

2. sprouted   b. grew

3. glee   c. charcoal-burning grill

4. pranced   d. danced about

5. *hibachi*   e. floor mat

THINKING CRITICALLY

1. Do you think the teakettle and the junkman make good living and business partners? Explain your answer.

2. Why do you think the priest changes his opinion about the kettle at the end of the story?

WRITING PROJECTS

1. Write either a magazine advertisement or a flyer that will persuade people to attend the street theater put on by the junkman and the teakettle.

2. Write the lyrics to a song for the teakettle to sing during its street theater performances. The song should tell about the adventures the teakettle has already had.

A MASON-DIXON MEMORY

by Clifton Davis

Sometimes it takes an unfortunate incident to show us how much our friends care. Even friends who rarely express their feelings may speak up for us in a time of need. When this happens, it can give us hope, despite the negative circumstances that brought about the need for the friends' expression of loyalty.

As a boy, Clifton Davis, the writer of this true story, was treated unfairly because of his ethnicity. What could have turned into a terrible situation takes an incredible twist because of the reaction of his friends. Thirty years later, while listening to a speech given by a high school student who had faced similar circumstances, Clifton remembers this important moment from his past.

VOCABULARY WORDS

provoked (prō·vōkt´) caused; led to
❖ His comment *provoked* excitement among the listeners.

forfeit (fôr´fit) to give up, lose, or be deprived of
❖ We had to *forfeit* the game because we did not have enough players.

chaperone (shap´ər·ōn´) a person who accompanies younger people at a gathering or on a trip
❖ The principal served as a *chaperone* at the school dance.

ominous (äm´ə·nəs) sinister; threatening
❖ The letter's *ominous* tone made the man feel uneasy.

discrimination (di·skrim´i·nā´shən) the act of treating people unfairly because they are different in some way
❖ Racial *discrimination* on public transportation is illegal.

caper (kā´pər) a foolish action or prank
❖ The girl's *caper* resulted in disciplinary action.

legislation (lej´is·lā´shən) a group of laws
❖ The president asked for *legislation* that would raise taxes.

bigotry (big´ə·trē) an attitude that shows one's dislike of people who are different
❖ Her *bigotry* against people from other countries is obvious.

Dondré Green glanced uneasily at the civic leaders and sports figures filling the hotel ballroom in Cleveland. They had come from across the nation to attend a fundraiser for the National Minority College Golf Scholarship Foundation. I was the banquet's featured entertainer. Dondré, an eighteen-year-old high school senior from Monroe, Louisiana, was the evening's honored guest.

"Nervous?" I asked the handsome young man in his starched white shirt and rented tuxedo.

"A little," he whispered, grinning.

One month earlier, Dondré had been just one more black student attending a predominantly white Southern school. Although most of his friends and classmates were white, Dondré's race had never been an issue. Then, on April 17, 1991, Dondré's black skin provoked an incident that made nationwide news.

"Ladies and gentlemen," the emcee said, "our special guest, Dondré Green."

As the audience stood applauding, Dondré walked to the microphone and began his story. "I love golf," he said quietly. "For the past two years, I've been a member of the St. Frederick High School golf team. And though I was the only black member, I've always felt at home playing at the mostly white country clubs across Louisiana."

The audience leaned forward; even the waiters and busboys stopped to listen. As I listened, a memory buried in my heart since childhood began fighting its way to life.

"Our team had driven from Monroe," Dondré continued. "When we arrived at the Caldwell Parish Country Club in Columbia, we walked to the putting green."

Dondré and his teammates were too absorbed to notice the conversation between a man and St. Frederick athletic director James Murphy. After disappearing into the clubhouse, Murphy returned to his players.

"I want to see the seniors," he said. "On the double!" His face seemed strained as he gathered the four students, including Dondré.

"I don't know how to tell you this," he said, "but the Caldwell Parish Country Club is reserved for whites only." Murphy paused and looked at Dondré. His teammates glanced at each other in disbelief. "I want you seniors to decide what our response should be," Murphy continued. "If we leave, we forfeit this tournament. If we stay, Dondré can't play."

As I listened, my own childhood memory from thirty-two years ago broke free.

In 1959 I was thirteen years old, a poor black kid living with my mother and stepfather in a small black ghetto on Long Island, New York. My mother worked nights in a hospital, and my stepfather drove a coal truck. Needless to say, our standard of living was somewhat short of the American dream.

Nevertheless, when my eighth-grade teacher announced a graduation trip to Washington, D.C., it never crossed my mind that I would be left behind. Besides a complete tour of the nation's capital, we would visit Glen Echo Amusement Park in Maryland. In my imagination, Glen Echo was Disneyland, Knott's Berry Farm, and Magic Mountain rolled into one.

My heart beating wildly, I raced home to deliver the mimeographed letter describing the journey. But when my mother saw how much the trip would cost, she just shook her head. We couldn't afford it.

After feeling sad for ten seconds, I decided to try to

fund the trip myself. For the next eight weeks, I sold candy bars door-to-door, delivered newspapers, and mowed lawns. Three days before the deadline, I'd made just barely enough. I was going!

The day of the trip, trembling with excitement, I climbed onto the train. I was the only nonwhite in our section.

Our hotel was not far from the White House. My roommate was Frank Miller, the son of a businessman. Leaning together out of our window and dropping water balloons on passing tourists quickly cemented our new friendship.

Every morning, almost a hundred of us loaded noisily onto our bus for another adventure. We sang our school fight song dozens of times—en route to Arlington National Cemetery and even on an afternoon cruise down the Potomac River.

We visited the Lincoln Memorial twice, once in daylight, the second time at dusk. My classmates and I fell silent as we walked in the shadows of those thirty-six marble columns, one for every state in the Union that Lincoln labored to preserve. I stood next to Frank at the base of the nineteen-foot seated statue. Spotlights made the white Georgian marble seem to glow. Together, we read those famous words from Lincoln's speech at Gettysburg, remembering the most bloody battle in the War Between the States: " . . . we here highly resolve that these dead shall not have died in vain—that this nation, under God, shall have a new birth of freedom. . . ."

As Frank motioned me into place to take my picture, I took one last look at Lincoln's face. He seemed alive and so terribly sad.

The next morning I understood a little better why he wasn't smiling. "Clifton," a chaperone said, "could I see you for a moment?"

The other guys at my table, especially Frank, turned pale. We had been joking about the previous night's direct water-balloon hit on a fat lady and her poodle. It was a stupid, dangerous act, but luckily nobody got hurt. We were celebrating our escape from punishment when the chaperone asked to see me.

"Clifton," she began, "so you know about the Mason-Dixon line?"

"No," I said, wondering what this had to do with drenching fat ladies.

"Before the Civil War," she explained, "the Mason-Dixon line was originally the boundary between Maryland and Pennsylvania—the dividing line between the slave and free states." Having escaped one disaster, I could feel another brewing. I noticed that her eyes were damp and her hands shaking.

"Today," she continued, "the Mason-Dixon line is a kind of invisible border between the North and the South. When you cross that invisible line out of Washington, D.C., into Maryland, things change."

There was an ominous drift to this conversation, but I wasn't following it. Why did she look and sound so nervous?

"Glen Echo Amusement Park is in Maryland," she said at last, "and the management doesn't allow Negroes inside." She stared at me in silence.

I was still grinning and nodding when the meaning finally sank in. "You mean I can't go to the park," I stuttered, "because I'm a Negro?"

She nodded slowly. "I'm sorry, Clifton," she said, taking my hand. "You'll have to stay in the hotel tonight. Why don't you and I watch a movie on television?"

I walked to the elevators feeling confusion, disbelief, anger, and a deep sadness. "What happened, Clifton?" Frank said when I got back to the room. "Did the fat lady tell on us?"

Without saying a word, I walked over to my bed, lay down, and began to cry. Frank was stunned into silence. Junior-high boys didn't cry, at least not in front of each other.

It wasn't just missing the class adventure that made me so sad. For the first time in my life, I was learning what it felt like to be a "nigger." Of course there was discrimination in the North, but the color of my skin had never officially kept me out of a coffee shop, a church—or an amusement park.

"Clifton," Frank whispered, "what is the matter?"

"They won't let me go to Glen Echo Park tonight," I sobbed.

"Because of the water balloon?" he asked.

"No," I answered, "because I'm a Negro."

"Well, that's a relief!" Frank said, and then he laughed, obviously relieved to have escaped punishment for our caper with the balloons. "I thought it was serious!"

Wiping away the tears with my sleeve, I stared at him. "It *is* serious. They don't let Negroes into the park. I can't go with you!" I shouted. "That's pretty serious to me."

I was about to wipe the silly grin off Frank's face with a blow to his jaw when I heard him say, "Then I won't go either."

For an instant we just froze. Then Frank grinned. I will never forget that moment. Frank was just a kid. He wanted to go to that amusement park as much as I did, but there was something even more important than the class night out. Still, he didn't explain or expand.

The next thing I knew, the room was filled with kids listening to Frank. "They don't allow Negroes in the park," he said, "so I'm staying with Clifton."

"Me too," a second boy said.

"Those jerks," a third muttered. "I'm with you, Clifton." My heart began to race. Suddenly I was not alone.

A pint-sized revolution had been born. The "water-balloon brigade," eleven white boys from Long Island, had made its decision: "We won't go." And as I sat on my bed in the center of it all, I felt grateful. But above all, I was filled with pride.

Dondré Green's story brought that childhood memory back to life. His golfing teammates, like my childhood friends, had an important decision to make. Standing by their friend would cost them dearly. But when it came time to decide, no one hesitated. "Let's get out of here," one of them whispered.

"They just turned and walked toward the van," Dondré told us. "They didn't debate it. And the younger players joined us without looking back."

Dondré was astounded by the response of his friends—and the people of Louisiana. The whole state was outraged and tried to make it right. The Louisiana House of Representatives proclaimed a Dondré Green Day and passed legislation permitting lawsuits for damages, attorneys' fees, and court costs against any private facility that invites a team, then bars any member because of race.

As Dondré concluded, his eyes glistened with tears. "I love my coach and my teammates for sticking by me," he said. "It goes to show that there are always good people who will not give in to bigotry. The kind of love they showed me that day will conquer hatred every time."

Suddenly the banquet crowd was standing, applauding Dondré Green.

My friends, too, had shown that kind of love. As we sat in the hotel, a chaperone came in waving an envelope. "Boys!" he shouted. "I've just bought thirteen tickets to the Senators–Tigers game. Anybody want to go?"

The room erupted in cheers. Not one of us had ever been to a professional baseball game in a real baseball park.

On the way to the stadium, we grew silent as our driver paused before the Lincoln Memorial. For one long moment, I stared through the marble pillars at Mr. Lincoln, bathed in that warm yellow light. There was still no smile and no sign of hope in his sad and tired eyes.

". . . we here highly resolve . . . that this nation, under God, shall have a new birth of freedom. . . . "

In his words and in his life, Lincoln had made it clear that freedom is not free. Every time the color of a person's skin keeps him out of an amusement park or off a country-club fairway, the war for freedom begins again. Sometimes the battle is fought with fists and guns, but more often the most effective weapon is a simple act of love and courage.

Whenever I hear those words from Lincoln's speech at Gettysburg, I remember my eleven white friends, and I feel hope once again. I like to imagine that when we paused that night at the foot of his great monument, Mr. Lincoln smiled at last. As Dondré said, "The kind of love they showed me that day will conquer hatred every time."

READING FOR UNDERSTANDING

1. Why is Dondré Green not allowed to play in the golf tournament held at the country club?

2. How does Clifton get the money to go on his school trip to Washington, D.C.?

3. How does Clifton feel when his classmates refuse to go to the amusement park without him?

4. How do Dondré's friends react to the news that he can't play at the country club?

5. What does Clifton consider to be the most effective weapon in the war for freedom?

RESPONDING TO THE STORY

Both Dondré's and Clifton's friends sacrificed something important to them to make a statement against discrimination. Do you know or have you heard or read about someone who has stood up for a friend who was being discriminated against? Describe this incident in a short paragraph.

REVIEWING VOCABULARY

1. Because the clouds looked *ominous*, the picnickers **(a)** decided to leave **(b)** unpacked the food basket **(c)** flew a kite.

2. When a feeling is *provoked*, it is **(a)** stirred up **(b)** denied **(c)** ignored.

3. My mother agreed to be a *chaperone* on my little brother's field trip because his class **(a)** stayed home **(b)** requires supervision **(c)** likes museums.

4. When the other school's team decided to *forfeit* the tennis match, our team automatically **(a)** lost **(b)** won **(c)** went home.

5. *Bigotry* often makes obvious a person's dislike for someone who is **(a)** like that person **(b)** different from that person **(c)** older than that person.

THINKING CRITICALLY

1. How do you think the chaperone feels when she tells Clifton he cannot go to the amusement park? Use details from the story to explain your answer.

2. Do you think that many students would react the way Dondré's and Clifton's classmates did? Explain your answer.

WRITING PROJECTS

1. Imagine that you are one of Clifton's friends. Write a letter to Clifton in which you explain why you chose to stay with him rather than go to the amusement park.

2. Write a newspaper editorial responding to the way the country club treated Dondré. In the editorial give reasons why this type of discrimination must end.

THE INTERLOPER
by Saki

Could you forgive your worst enemy? Though it is only human to become angry with people if they do something that you think is unfair, most people are able to forgive. When people do not learn the art of forgiveness, their anger often grows and can become dangerous.

The refusal to forgive is at the center of the hatred shared by Ulrich von Gradwitz and Georg Znaeym. These men have carried their families' mutual grudges for years. Now, in one night, as near tragedy strikes them, they have the chance to make a new start. Do they have the courage to put the past behind them? Read the story to find out.

VOCABULARY WORDS

game (gām) wild animals, birds, or fish hunted for food or sport

❖ The family liked to hunt *game* for Thanksgiving dinner.

feud (fyo͞od) a bitter, long-lasting quarrel

❖ The *feud* between the Hatfields and the McCoys has lasted for many years.

oaths (ōths) swear words

❖ He yelled out the *oath* "Drat!" when he dropped the heavy cement block on his toes.

regrets (ri gretz´) expressions of disappointment or sadness

❖ Nadia sent her *regrets* for not being able to attend the party.

meddle (med´l) to interfere in

❖ Brian learned not to *meddle* in other people's business.

 **In a forest somewhere** in the eastern Carpathians, a man stood. It was a winter night. He watched and listened like a man who is hunting. But the game he looked for was not usually hunted. Ulrich von Gradwitz searched the dark forest for a human enemy.

The forests of von Gradwitz were large and well supplied with game. The small strip of steep woods on its border, however, was not known for good hunting.

There was not much game. But it was the most carefully guarded area of von Gradwitz's land.

A famous lawsuit, in the days of von Gradwitz's grandfather, took it from a neighbor. The neighbor was a small landowner with no legal right to the land. They lost the case. But they did not agree with the Court's ruling. As a result, there were many fights that followed over hunting rights. It caused a bitter feeling between the families. This feeling lasted for three generations.

The feud became personal once Ulrich became head of his family. The man he hated most in the world was Georg Znaeym. Znaeym was the head of the neighboring family. The feud might have died down. The families might have reached an agreement. But both men continued to fight each other. As boys, they thirsted for each other's blood. As men, each prayed bad luck might fall on the other.

On this windy winter night, Ulrich called together his men to watch the dark forest. They were to keep a lookout for prowling thieves. The deer usually kept under cover during a storm. Tonight, however, these creatures were uneasy. Instead of sleeping as usual, they were running like driven things. Clearly there was something troubling in the forest. Ulrich could guess from where it came.

He walked away by himself. The men on lookout duty were waiting on the crest of the hill. Ulrich wandered far down the steep slopes into the wild tangle of bushes. He looked through the tree trunks for sight or sound of the thieves. He thought to himself what it might be like if he came across his enemy, Georg Znaeym. To meet him alone, that was his chief thought. And as he stepped round the trunk of a huge tree, he came face to face with the man he wanted to see.

The two enemies stood glaring at one another for a long, silent moment. Each held a rifle. Each had hate in his heart and murder on his mind. The chance had come to play out the hatred of a lifetime. But a civilized man cannot easily bring himself to shoot down his neighbor. One kills in cold blood and without a word only for a crime against his home and honor.

While the men hesitated, there was a splitting crash over their heads. Before they could leap aside, a huge falling tree thundered down on them. Ulrich von Gradwitz found himself stretched on the ground. One arm lay numb beneath him. The other was held in a tangle of branches. Both legs were pinned beneath the fallen mass. His heavy boots had saved his feet from being crushed. His broken bones were not as serious as they might have been. Yet it was clear that he could not move till someone came to free him. The falling twigs had slashed the skin of his face. He winked away some drops of blood from his eyelashes. Only then could he get a view of the disaster.

At his side lay Georg Znaeym. He was so close to Ulrich, the two men could have touched. Georg Znaeym was alive. He was also helplessly trapped. All round the men lay thick piles of splintered branches and broken twigs.

The men were glad to be alive. But they were angry at being trapped. It brought on mixed feelings. Solemn thanks and sharp oaths came to Ulrich's lips. Georg was nearly blinded by blood dripping across his eyes. He stopped struggling for a moment. He listened. Then he gave a short, mad laugh.

"So you're not killed as you ought to be. But you're caught, anyway," Georg cried. "Caught fast. Ha! What a joke. Ulrich von Gradwitz is trapped in his stolen forest. There's justice for you!"

He laughed again.

"I'm caught in my own forest land," returned Ulrich. "When my men come to free us, you will wish you were in some other spot. Caught hunting on a neighbor's land. Shame on you."

Georg was silent for a moment. Then he answered quietly.

"Are you sure your men will find much to free? I have men, too. They were in the forest tonight. They will be here first. They will do the freeing. They will drag me out from under these branches. With a little clumsiness on their part, they might roll this huge trunk on you. Your men will find you dead. To make it look good, I will send my regrets to your family."

"Good," snarled Georg, "good. We'll fight this out to the death. You, I, and our men. No outsiders will come between us. Death and hell's fires to you, Ulrich von Gradwitz."

"The same to you, Georg Znaeym," said Ulrich. "Land thief, game grabber."

Both men spoke with the bitter possibility of losing. Each knew that it might be a long time before his men found him. It was a plain case of who would come first.

Both had given up the useless struggle to get free. The mass of wood held them down. Ulrich tried only to bring one partly free arm to his coat. He hoped to reach his water. Even after he reached it, it was a long time before he got any water down his throat. But what a heaven-sent swallow it was! It was winter, and little snow had fallen as yet. Because of this, the captives suffered less from the cold than might be expected. Even so, the water was refreshing to the injured man. He looked across at his enemy with a small throb of pity. Georg could just barely keep the groans of pain and weariness from his lips.

"Could you reach this water if I threw it over to you?" asked Ulrich suddenly. "One should be as well off as possible."

"No, I can hardly see anything. There is so much blood caked around my eyes," said Georg. "In any case I don't take water from an enemy."

Ulrich was silent for a few minutes. He lay listening to the low whistle of the wind. An idea was slowly growing in his brain. It became stronger every time he looked across the branches. In the pain Ulrich was feeling, his old hatred seemed to be dying.

"Neighbor," he said at last. "Do as you please if your men come first. It was a fair deal. But as for me, I've changed my mind. If my men come first, you shall be the first to be helped. You will be treated as my guest. We have fought like devils all our lives. Fought over this stupid strip of forest. A place where the trees can't even stand up in the wind. Lying here tonight, thinking, I've learned we've been fools. There are better things in life than winning a quarrel over land. Neighbor, if you will help me to bury the old quarrel, I—I will ask you to be my friend."

Georg Znaeym was silent for a long time. Ulrich thought perhaps he had fainted from his injuries. Then Georg spoke slowly and in jerks.

"How the market square would stare and talk if we rode into the town square together. No one living can remember seeing a Znaeym and a von Gradwitz having a friendly talk. What peace there would be among the

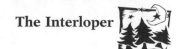

forest folk if we were to end our feud. If we were to make peace among our people, no outsider could meddle. You would spend nights under my roof.

I would feast with you at your castle. I would never fire a shot on your land except as your guest. You could shoot with me down in the marshes where the wild birds are. In all the countryside, none could stop us if we chose to make peace. I thought I would hate you all my life. Now I think I have changed my mind about things. You offered me water. . . . Ulrich von Gradwitz, I will be your friend."

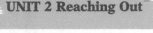

READING FOR UNDERSTANDING

1. Why do Georg and Ulrich hate each other?
2. What happens to the two men when they come face to face in the forest?
3. How do Georg and Ulrich plan to get free?
4. Why does Ulrich offer water to his enemy?
5. What does Georg say would happen if he and Ulrich ended their feud?

RESPONDING TO THE STORY

Ulrich von Gradwitz and Georg Znaeym have been bitter enemies since they were born. When faced with a life-threatening situation, however, they decide to put aside their differences and become friends. Have you ever been in a situation where you and someone you didn't get along with had to put your differences aside? In a short paragraph, explain what happened.

REVIEWING VOCABULARY

1. The family *feud* made the children of each family **(a)** hate each other **(b)** like each other **(c)** forget each other.

2. His mother said that if he chose to *meddle* his friends might think he was **(a)** uncaring **(b)** helpful **(c)** nosy.

3. The boy shouted out an *oath* when he made a(n) **(a)** goal **(b)** error **(c)** high grade.

4. It is polite to express *regrets* after something has happened that is **(a)** good **(b)** fair **(c)** unfortunate.

5. A good example of wild *game* is **(a)** checkers **(b)** football **(c)** a turkey.

THINKING CRITICALLY

1. Why do you think Georg and Ulrich carried on their families' hatred for each other when it had nothing to do with them individually?

2. How would you explain why Georg and Ulrich decided to forgive each other?

WRITING PROJECTS

1. Imagine that you and your friends have just witnessed Ulrich and Georg ride into the town square together for the first time. Write the conversation that you and your friends have at seeing this surprising occurrence.

2. Write a newspaper article describing the ending of the feud between the von Gradwitz and the Znaeym families.

"*We mutually pledge to each other our lives, our fortunes, and our sacred honor.*" — Thomas Jefferson

Unit 3
A COMMON PURPOSE

HOW WAR WAS ENDED

retold by Heather Forest

Where do you turn when you have an important problem to solve? We often try to solve problems in ways that have been used before, even when those ways have not worked well in the past. It takes a brave, creative person to try something different. Even for such a person, sometimes the solution to a problem comes in an unexpected way.

The Yup'ik people of central Alaska have a serious problem. Warring groups are repeatedly attacking the Yup'ik homes, making normal life impossible. The Yup'ik hope that their brave warrior, Apanugpak, will fight off the attackers. Yet Apanugpak, in the tale you are about to read, has the courage to challenge his people with a new idea.

VOCABULARY WORDS

renowned (ri nound´) well-known and respected
❖ The artist was *renowned* by art lovers everywhere.

subterranean (sub´tə rā´nē ən) underground
❖ The well water came from a *subterranean* stream.

tundra (tun´drə) flat, treeless landscape of the arctic regions
❖ The warriors from Alaska marched for days across the frozen *tundra*.

futile (fyo͞ot´´l) pointless; hopeless
❖ Their efforts to find gold were *futile*; their investment was a failure.

vanquish (vang´kwish) to overcome or defeat
❖ Her arguments could *vanquish* any opponent in a debate.

discord (dis´kôrd´) conflict; disagreement
❖ The coach tried to settle the *discord* among the players.

prevailed (prē vāld´) won, was the strongest
❖ Fortunately, his good idea *prevailed* over all the other ideas in the meeting.

savory (sā´vər ē) appetizing
❖ The *savory* aroma of the soup made my mouth water.

Five hundred years before the first outsiders came to central Alaska, there lived a powerful Yup'ik warrior named Apanugpak. He was renowned by the Yup'ik people for his skill with the harpoon and bow and arrow.

It was a time of great madness and terror among the Yup'ik. Warring groups attacked each other across the tundra. People lived in fear within their subterranean sod houses, unable to safely light fires or to cook food. Each band of warriors had a "smeller" who traveled with them. The "smellers" had such keen noses they could sense even one particle of smoke in the pristine air of the cold tundra and direct the warriors to the source of the fire. People were cold, hungry, and afraid.

It came to pass that one day Apanugpak had a vision. In the vision he saw houses in villages everywhere vanishing into the sky as curling wisps of black smoke. He saw a crimson lake of blood, made from the dripping wounds of slain warriors. As he gazed at these strange sights, Apanugpak, the bravest of warriors, was struck with terror. He trembled as he watched the ghosts of dead warriors slowly rise up to do battle with the living.

At that moment, Apanugpak knew that war was futile. No side could win, for as warriors killed more and more people, the vast army of ghosts would continue to increase. Like memories of horror driving people to revenge, the ghosts of war would vanquish the living and cause great suffering to continue endlessly. Apanugpak knew then that war must end.

He was the most respected of all the fierce warriors. People were surprised when he held up his harpoon and his bow and arrows and said, "These things were created to help us hunt for food, not to cause death to each other. I will not use these tools to fight people any longer." When Apanugpak, the greatest warrior, put down his weapons, all the others followed. The time of madness was over. The killing was finished.

Discord between people found a different expression. People created new kinds of contests. Instead of killing each other in battle, warring bands began to compete energetically with each other in singing contests, dancing contests, and insulting contests. Colorful gatherings rich in music, movement, and pointed, clever words settled disputes.

Peace prevailed and people were able to light their hearth fires again. The sweet smell of savory food, cooking in subterranean homes, signaled the return of sanity to the land of ice and cold.

READING FOR UNDERSTANDING

1. With what weapons is the warrior Apanugpak skilled?

2. What is the cause of the madness and terror among the Yup'ik?

3. What is the function of the "smeller" in Yup'ik society?

4. What does Apanugpak's vision show him about war?

5. What do the people do when war ends?

RESPONDING TO THE STORY

Apanugpak is famous as a warrior. Yet after he has a vision that shows him how horrible and useless war is, he has the courage to stop fighting. Do you know or have you heard or read about someone who has had the courage to take action to benefit others? In a short paragraph, explain how he or she acted courageously.

REVIEWING VOCABULARY

1. When the candidate we voted for *prevailed*, he was (a) embarrassed (b) sent away (c) elected.

2. To *vanquish* starvation in poor countries, the charity organization (a) sends food (b) builds cars (c) eats more.

3. When the angry protesters showed up at the courthouse, there was much *discord* and (a) happiness (b) quiet (c) shouting.

4. Andrea realized that lying is *futile* so she (a) told many lies (b) told the truth (c) told a joke.

5. People stood in line for hours to meet the *renowned* author because they (a) feel sorry for her (b) want to help her (c) admire her work.

THINKING CRITICALLY

1. Apanugpak brings an end to war by putting down his weapons. Do you think Apanugpak acts courageously? Why or why not?

2. Do you think having contests is a good way to settle disagreements? Explain your answer.

WRITING PROJECTS

1. Write a speech that Apanugpak will give to explain his new stand against war. The speech should include ideas that will persuade other warriors to follow his example.

2. Imagine that you are a member of the Yup'ik community. Write a letter to Apanugpak explaining your feelings about his decision to give up war.

THE SHEEP OF SAN CRISTÓBAL
by Terri Bueno

Hundreds of years ago, when New Mexico belonged to Spain, the settlers and the Ute Indians fought over the land. One day a Spanish woman, Felipa, returns home from the fields to find that the Utes have kidnapped her seven-year-old son! Although she has no hope of getting him back, Felipa prays for the strength to go on living.

Felipa has another problem: A neighbor has been letting his sheep eat her bean crop. The sheep eat all the beans, leaving Felipa without a way to earn money. Wild with anger, she calls on the saint of travelers, San Cristóbal (Saint Christopher), to throw this neighbor off the mesa! When it really happens, Felipa feels she must make up for her evil thoughts. The unselfish way she embraces her punishment by performing acts of charity brings her a great reward, one that she would never have expected.

149

VOCABULARY WORDS

mesa (māˊsə) a small piece of flat land that is higher than the land around it
❖ The *mesa* stretched out flat before her.

fatuous (fachōō əs) silly; foolish
❖ The boy had a *fatuous* grin on his face as he watched the television program.

reproachful (ri prōchˊfəl) expressing blame
❖ The mother gave a *reproachful* look to her son when he brought home a bad report card.

penance (penˊəns) something that is done to make up for a wrongdoing
❖ The girl washed the family car as *penance* for not studying for her test.

indigent (inˊdi jənt) in poverty; poor; needy
❖ The *indigent* man had no home and nothing to eat.

ewe (yōō) a female sheep
❖ Only a *ewe* can give birth to a lamb.

emaciated (ē māˊsē ātˊid) abnormally thin, usually as a result of starvation or disease
❖ Many of the children in that country do not get enough to eat and are *emaciated*.

adobe (ə dōˊbē) a building made of sun-dried bricks
❖ Some people in the Southwest live in *adobe* homes.

In the days that followed, deep sorrow never left Felipa . . . But little by little, she learned to do what she had to do. She had always been very religious, and now she spent at least an hour a day on her knees at the shrine. The rest of the time she worked in her field—digging, planting, hoeing, picking.

Sometimes she carried a basket of vegetables to the center of Las Colonias to sell. The people of the little town had always liked Felipa, and now they felt sorry for her. They would buy from her first. Men who cut firewood often dropped off a few pieces as they went by her doorstep. Other people did her other little favors, and Felipa always remembered to thank them.

There was one man, however, whose favors Felipa did not want. This was Don José Vigil. From his father, Don José had inherited a huge flock of sheep. People said he was the richest man in town, but people also knew that he never gave anything to the poor. It was not Don José's habit to help anyone but himself. Felipa soon learned the reason for his favors to her: He was a young man without a wife, and she was a young woman without a husband.

At night Don José kept his sheep in a corral beside his house in town. In the daytime he took them to the top of a huge mesa to eat grass. This meant that twice a day, morning and evening, Don José had to pass Felipa's house with his sheep. Felipa would groan when she saw them coming up the dirt road. Leading the way would be Sancho, Don José's big dog; then would come the sheep, and finally Don José himself. Always he would smile and stop to talk.

Felipa did nothing to lead Don José on—but he would not be stopped. If she would not talk to him, he would talk for both of them. If she refused a present, he would leave it on the ground. If she hid in the house, he would simply open the door and walk in. Only if she locked the door would Don José leave, angry and silent. Felipa didn't like making anyone mad, but locking the door was better than listening to all his fatuous talk of marriage.

Soon Felipa found herself locking the door twice a day. And to her surprise, she sometimes found herself thinking evil thoughts about Don José. "If only Don José would fall off the mesa and break his neck!" she would think. Then, realizing how mean her thoughts had been, she would sigh and pray to Our Lady for forgiveness.

Before long, however, Don José found a way to get Felipa out of her house. He changed places with Sancho, the big brown dog. Instead of having Sancho lead the sheep, he led them himself. When he got to Felipa's house, he stopped. For a few minutes the sheep would stand still on the road. But soon, left to themselves, they would wander into Felipa's field. They would begin to eat her half-grown bean plants. Felipa had no choice. She would come tearing out of the house, shouting and waving her arms at the sheep, as Don José stood in the road and laughed.

The same thing happened every morning for a week. Felipa was puzzled. What was Don José trying to do? Was he trying to punish her for not liking him? Was he trying to force her to marry him? Without the beans to sell, Felipa would soon have no money. Then what would she do? What could she do?

One morning Don José's sheep arrived very early. Waking up to hear them already in her field, Felipa quickly looked out the window. They were eating the last of the beans.

Wild with anger, Felipa bolted out of the house. First she screamed at the sheep. But what was the use? Her beans had already disappeared. Then she screamed at Don José:

"You are a bad man, Don José Vigil! A bad man! May San Cristóbal throw you off the mesa today! May he break your neck! May you—"

Bursting into tears, Felipa ran back into the house. The door slammed behind her. She didn't watch as Don José shook his head, laughed once, and followed the last of his sheep toward the mesa. The peaceful dog Sancho was already way ahead.

Four hours later, the body of Don José Vigil was carried past Felipa's house. His foot had landed on the wrong small round stone on the narrow path up the side of the mesa. He had slipped, fallen to the plain far below, and broken his neck.

The news made Felipa feel dead herself. Her anger turned inward, toward herself. She was sure that her curse had caused Don José's death. All day long she prayed to Nuestra Señora de los Dolores, Our Lady of Sorrows. She could eat nothing, and that night she could not sleep. She kept seeing the reproachful eyes of Don José as he fell to his death. They seemed to look right at her, and they made her feel very guilty.

Early the next morning, Felipa hurried to the church. There was only one thing to do. She would have to ask for penance, for some kind of punishment that would make up for her evil words.

"Padre," Felipa whispered to the priest. "I am guilty of the death of Don José Vigil." Then she sobbingly told the whole story.

"No," the priest finally said, "you did not cause Don José to die. San Cristóbal would not listen to such a plea. He would not do such a thing. He would never listen to a wicked prayer made by an angry woman."

The old priest looked into Felipa's big brown eyes and went on: "But yes, you are guilty. You are guilty of a very wicked prayer. And for that evil act, you must do penance."

"Yes," murmured Felipa, "I know. Without the penance, the rest of my life would be empty."

"Here is what you must do," the priest told her. "You must do penance for your own evil wishes. But more important, you must do penance for Don José, too. You see, he was in some ways an evil man. He had much money, yet he never gave to the poor. But no man is all evil. Right now, could he join us again on earth, Don José would want to do good. That is why your penance must be for him also."

Felipa listened as the priest went on. First she was to go to the mesa and gather Don José's sheep together. Then she was to drive them all over New Mexico, to every village. Everywhere she went, she was to search for indigent people in real need. To each of these people she was to give a single sheep. Felipa was to give the sheep away in the name of Don José, with the blessing of San Cristóbal. She was to beg for bread and eat nothing else. She was to carry only a cup and use it only for sheep milk.

"If anyone asks you," the priest finished, "say that the sheep are the sheep of San Cristóbal. Have faith, my daughter. San Cristóbal will guide you. Pray often. And at the end, he will give you a sign. You will know that your penance is over, and that you are free of your sin."

Felipa did as she'd been told. First she went to her house to get a cup. Should she change her clothes? No, she decided. She'd keep on what she'd worn to the church, a simple black robe with a hood. Then she headed for the mesa. Her whole body shook as she walked up the dangerous path where Don José had fallen.

On the mesa's flat top, she found the sheep in a group. The faithful dog Sancho had kept them together during the night.

Sancho barked with joy when he saw Felipa coming. He ran up and nuzzled his short brown nose against her leg. Then he led her into some bushes not far away. There on the ground, Felipa saw the bones of three lambs. She knew that coyotes must have taken them during the night.

"You are a good, good dog, Sancho," Felipa scratched the big brown head by her knee. "But some lambs have been lost, am I right? You could not do the whole job, could you? Now you have me to help you. And I have you to help me."

Felipa milked one of the sheep. She held the cup of milk out to Sancho, and he lapped it up quickly. Then they drove the sheep toward the path leading off the mesa. Once safely down, and with Sancho leading, they headed for town. Felipa passed her own house, wondering when she'd ever see it again. A few minutes later they came to the house of Don José. Sancho started to drive the sheep into the corral, as he had always done. Felipa ran forward and headed the sheep back onto the road. She pulled the corral gate shut and urged the sheep on by. Sancho stood next to the corral, his head tipped to one side.

Now the sheep were past Don José's house, and almost to the center of Las Colonias. Felipa looked back at Don José's corral. Sancho was still standing there, watching her.

"Come, Sancho!" Felipa called. "Come! Come!" She clapped her hands together.

For a moment Sancho didn't move. Then all at once he seemed to make up his mind. He rushed toward Felipa, passed her, and took his place far up, in front of the sheep.

The sheep moved through Las Colonias and headed out of town. Felipa tried to count them. Because they were moving and close together, it wasn't an easy job. The first time she counted 172. The second time she got 167. Then she noticed that a large black ewe had dropped back to walk at her side. An hour later, the ewe was still there. Felipa looked at the animal carefully. "I think this sheep wants to be milked," she told herself. "She must be one of the ewes who lost their lambs to the coyotes."

Coming to a grassy spot, Felipa decided that it was time for the whole procession to rest. As the other sheep browsed, Felipa milked the large black ewe. She drank the first cup of warm milk herself. The second she gave to Sancho. That was all, and the ewe then wandered off to graze on the thin grass. But as soon as they started down the dusty road again, the ewe came back to Felipa's side.

"You are a good friend, black ewe," Felipa said aloud. "Do you know that I too have lost a child? Can you tell that I share your sadness? Is that why you stay here next to me?"

Before the sun set that day, Felipa had given the black ewe a name: Negrita. In the evening Felipa milked her again, and again the ewe moved away to eat. But as it got dark, and the rest of the sheep settled down for the night, Negrita came back to Felipa and lay down. Felipa lay down, too, using Negrita's soft side as a pillow. She knew that Sancho would stay half awake and watch the sheep.

Soon Felipa was sound asleep. Later she dreamed of Don José's face—smiling at her.

Early the next morning the journey continued, with Negrita still at Felipa's side. About noon they got to the first town, San José. Felipa was surprised to find that everyone was waiting for her. The news of her penance and her journey had traveled on ahead. Many people offered her bread, more than she could have eaten in a week. She asked and asked, but she could find no one poor enough to be given a sheep.

The same reception greeted Felipa in the next village, except that there she gave away her first sheep. And in the town after that she had the same experience. Continuing on, everywhere she went, she found that people had heard of her. On the third day her shoes wore out, and at first the dry desert sand hurt her feet. But she kept going. She traveled down the Rio Grande valley, where she found many poor people. Once she discovered a wrinkled old Indian woman who was starving in a mud hut. "In the name of Don José, and with the blessing of San Cristóbal, I give you this large sheep," Felipa told her. She knew without asking that the woman was a Ute.

The days turned into weeks, and the weeks turned into months. Felipa walked through Santa Cruz, headed north to Chimayo, and then south toward Pogoáqua. Nearly every day, she gave away a sheep. The number of sheep grew smaller and smaller. She went past Tesúque, then over the hills to Santa Fe. Finally there were only a few sheep left. There was no need for Sancho to lead them. He now walked on one side of Felipa, with the good sheep Negrita on the other.

In Albuquerque, Felipa gave away her next-to-last sheep. Now only Negrita was left. The next town, Felipa knew, was Bajada, and for the first time she didn't want to go on. She prayed that there would be no one in La Bajada poor enough to deserve a sheep. But she also knew that if she found the right person, even Negrita would have to go.

Negrita did have to go. Felipa offered her to an emaciated old man who lay on a mat in the shade of a tree. He was almost too weak to stand up.

"Good-bye, Negrita," Felipa said. "You have been a good friend. Good-bye. Good-bye. Good-bye."

As the old man took hold of Negrita, Felipa got down on her knees. She buried her face in Negrita's soft neck. Suddenly feeling tears come to her eyes, she stood up quickly and turned to leave. But all at once, there was Negrita at her side again. The old man had not been strong enough to hold her.

"No, Negrita!" Felipa said. Now the tears were on her cheeks. "You must stay here!" She found a piece of rope and tied Negrita to the tree next to the old man. But when she again started to leave, a strange thing happened. Sancho stayed behind. He growled at the old man; then he growled at Negrita. Suddenly he started to bark. He ran at Negrita, sinking his sharp teeth into one of her back legs. The rope broke, and in an instant both animals were back at Felipa's side.

What should she do? Take Negrita back to the man again? No, Felipa decided. Perplexed, she walked on in silence. She could not force herself to return Negrita to the old man once more. But how long, really, could she keep Negrita? The next village was Socorro (which at the time was the last town in lower New Mexico). Surely, someone there would be poor enough to deserve the last of San Cristóbal's sheep.

Felipa entered Socorro with a heavy heart. As usual, the people already knew she was on her way. They offered her bread and answered her questions. No, they said, there was really no one poor enough to get a sheep. But Felipa didn't feel quite sure that everyone was telling the truth. She then looked into every house. She held her breath at every doorway, but she found no one poor enough to deserve Negrita.

Beyond the town, on the edge of the desert, was one old house. It was a hut, really, adobe, poles, and animal skins. Felipa, with Negrita and Sancho by her side, approached it slowly. A tall man stepped out and stood at the doorway. His face mirrored the hue of the sun-baked desert sand. His wide-brimmed hat was filled with holes, and his clothes were rags.

"Certainly," Felipa told herself, "this is the person."

"In the name of Don José, and with the blessing of San Cristóbal—" Felipa began.

"Ah!" said the man. "So you are Felipa Sandoval!"

Felipa nodded. She watched the man as he smiled at her suddenly.

"No," he said, shaking his head slowly. "You will not give your last sheep to me. I am getting old, but I can still work. I am not as poor as I look."

Felipa's heart rose—then began to plummet again as the man went on:

"You should give your sheep to the child in my hut. He seems to be really in need. I got him from some Navajo Indians yesterday, for just a piece of cheap turquoise. The Navajos told me they got him from the Utes."

Felipa went into the hut. There in the shadows, dressed in Indian clothing, stood her son Manuel.

Feeling her head swimming, Felipa fell to her knees. Was it true? . . .

The boy ran toward her arms, and Felipa knew it was true.

This was her son. Her only son. Her son Manuel. She had not held him close to her in a little more than a year.

Bark, bark—it was the dog Sancho, from outside the hut. Felipa pulled the boy toward the door, and stepped outside. Negrita came up and nuzzled Felipa's leg as she stood blinking in the bright sunlight. Where was the man? She walked around the hut. Had he simply vanished?

Felipa hurried back to the center of Socorro. She asked about the tall stranger. Even though she described him clearly, the people in town said they had never seen such a man. The hut, they said, had been built years before for goats. No one had ever lived in it. Now even the goats had given it up.

Suddenly Felipa stopped listening. She knew intuitively who the man had been. She knew that San Cristóbal himself had delivered her little boy to her. And she knew, too, as the cloud of her guilt left her, that her penance was over.

For many years, people in New Mexico talked about Felipa Sandoval. They remembered her long walk with the sheep to Socorro. And they remembered even better her journey back home. No one ever forgot the young woman with the kind and joyful face, the little boy, the brown dog, and the black ewe.

Back in Las Colonias, Felipa found only happiness. Her neighbors had cared for her field, and beans were ready to be picked. She and Manuel picked them in peace, happy to be home, and not really caring that their story spread throughout the whole Southwest and then to the rest of the country.

READING FOR UNDERSTANDING

1. Why does Don José Vigil pay so much attention to Felipa?

2. Why does Felipa curse Don José?

3. How will Felipa know when her penance is over?

4. What happens when Felipa ties Negrita to a tree beside the thin old man?

5. What does Felipa find when she finally returns home?

RESPONDING TO THE STORY

Felipa undertakes a journey for her penance that results in performing acts of charity. In a short paragraph, describe an act of charity you or someone you know or have heard or read about performed and what the inspiration was for doing it.

REVIEWING VOCABULARY

Match each word on the left with the correct definition on the right.

1. indigent

    a. something that is done to make up for a wrongdoing

2. penance

    b. expressing blame

3. emaciated

    c. silly; foolish

4. reproachful

    d. in poverty; poor; needy

5. fatuous

    e. abnormally thin, usually as a result of starvation or disease

THINKING CRITICALLY

1. Why do you think the people who live in the villages Felipa visits are so kind and generous toward her?

2. Why do you think Felipa's story spreads throughout the Southwest and the country?

WRITING PROJECTS

1. Imagine that you were one of the indigent people to whom Felipa gave a sheep. Write a letter to her thanking her for the gift and explaining how it changed your life.

2. Write two paragraphs comparing the actions of Felipa and those of Don José.

Navajo Code Talker
as told to Ricky Begay by Joe Bennett, his grandfather

How far would you be willing to go to serve your country? "Navajo Code Talker" reveals the experiences of Joe Bennett, who joins the Marines when he is only 15 years old. Joe is proud of his United States citizenship and wants to help his country during World War II by joining other Navajos who are being trained to speak in a secret code based on the Navajo language. As a code talker, Joe faces the same dangers faced by any other soldier. Yet he welcomes this opportunity to play a special role in his country's history.

Joe's memories are part of an unusual book—one created by a group of students in Albuquerque, New Mexico, who wanted to raise money to buy a peace statue for their school. Joe's story of citizenship and service to his country is one example of the stories, interviews, and other information the children collected to reflect their community.

VOCABULARY WORDS

reservation (rez´ ər vā´shən) public land set aside for a special use; land set aside by the U.S. government for Native American citizens

❖ Some Native Americans live on *reservations*.

crack (krak) to manage to solve

❖ The detective was able to *crack* the safe's combination.

combat zone (käm´bat´ zōn) an area where armed fighting takes place

❖ Many soldiers were wounded in the *combat zone*.

division (də vizh´ən) a major military unit that can act independently and is under one command

❖ The armored *division* was assigned to Normandy.

foxhole (fäks´hōl´) a hole dug in the ground as a temporary protection for soldiers against enemy gunfire

❖ We took cover in the *foxhole* when we saw the tanks approaching.

acknowledge (ak näl´ij) to state that one has received something

❖ You should *acknowledge* the gift with a thank-you card.

My name is Joe Bennett, age sixty-five. I grew up on the Navajo Indian Reservation near Shiprock, New Mexico. I was fifteen when the Japanese bombed Pearl Harbor at the start of World War II. I was herding my family's sheep when a couple of Marines came to the reservation, looking for young men who could speak English and Navajo. They wanted us to join the Marines and be trained to talk in a new code that the Japanese would not be able to crack. They thought the Navajo language was so hard it would fool the enemy. They were right.

I wanted to be a code talker, so I lied and said I was eighteen. Next thing I knew, I was on a train going to San Diego. Never been away from the reservation, never seen a train, didn't know what was going on. It was like a dream. Didn't have sense enough to be scared. I learned that later.

The Marines were afraid the Japanese might find somebody who understood Navajo, even though it's such a hard language. So they had the men make up a Navajo code. They figured out 211 words, plus a word for each letter of the alphabet. Each word stood for something different from what it means in our language. For instance, our word for "whale" is *lotso*, and that is the word they decided to use for "battleship." They kept adding more and more words with mixed-up meanings. We had to memorize what all those words meant. It was a good code. The Japanese never did crack it.

I was shipped to Guadalcanal. At first the officers didn't know what to do with the code talkers. Then they learned to depend on us. By the end of the war there were about four hundred code talkers. It was dangerous work, and some got killed. One of the big dangers was not from the Japanese. Sometimes the white Marines mistook the Navajos for Japanese spies and wanted to kill us. So a white soldier was sent along as a kind of bodyguard for each code talker in the combat zone.

There were usually two code talkers in each division. One went ashore and the other stayed on the ship. We used our radios to send the officers' messages back and forth, coding and decoding them fast.

I took part in the invasion of Iwo Jima. That was one of the most important battles in the war. The invasion was directed by orders in Navajo code. We sent more than eight hundred messages, but the Japanese were not able to figure out a single one.

I was sent ashore with a white Marine. We tied ourselves together with a piece of rope so we wouldn't get separated in the dark. We crawled into a foxhole. But then the white Marine got hit, and I had to stay in the foxhole with the dead man and keep sending messages back to the ship. It was hard because Navajo people are afraid of dead bodies.

When I came home after the war, I and other Navajo soldiers had an "Enemy Way" ceremony to get rid of the bad memories and the ghosts of the dead that haunted us.

For a long time after the war, the code talkers were kept a secret. But we had a fiftieth anniversary celebration at the Pentagon. I went to Washington, D.C., for the celebration. I didn't think I could still remember the code because I'm old and it was all a long time ago, but when somebody sent the message "Give back the ram" in Navajo, I knew what it meant: Acknowledge message.

I am proud of the Navajo code talkers and glad I could serve my country.

READING FOR UNDERSTANDING

1. Why did the Marines choose the Navajo language for their code?

2. What was one of the biggest dangers the code talkers faced?

3. How did the code talkers in each division operate?

4. In what kind of ceremonies and celebrations did the Navajo code talkers participate after the war?

5. How do you think the the Navajo code helped the United States to win the war?

RESPONDING TO THE STORY

Joe Bennett helped his country during a time of war by working as a Navajo code talker. Name and describe some other ways that people are able to help their country on a daily basis.

REVIEWING VOCABULARY

Fill in each blank with the correct word from the following list: *division, combat zone, reservation, crack, acknowledge.*

1. Many helicopters were sent into the _____ to rescue injured soldiers.

2. The private investigator is trying to _____ the case of the missing jewels.

3. The shipping clerk called to _____ that she received the package.

4. Charles brought back a beautifully painted clay pot from his trip to the Hopi _____ .

5. The cavalry _____ rode horses into battle.

THINKING CRITICALLY

1. Why do you think that Joe Bennett wanted to be a Navajo code talker badly enough to lie about his age?

2. Why do you think that Joe Bennett told his grandson about his experiences as a Navajo code talker?

WRITING PROJECTS

1. Write a newspaper article telling the story of Joe Bennett and the Navajo code talkers.

2. Write a letter to Joe Bennett or a service member that you know expressing your appreciation of his or her dedication and service to the country.

THE OLD MAN OF THE FLOWERS

retold by Yoshiko Uchida

When something wonderful happens to you, what is the first thing you do? Most of us immediately share the good news with others. Sharing our good fortune often brings us just as much joy as the good fortune itself.

The old man and woman in this folktale enjoy sharing the gifts they acquire through the actions of their beloved dog with their neighbor and their community. Unfortunately, the neighbor does not react to their generosity in a way you would expect. Read on to find out how this issue is resolved.

VOCABULARY WORDS

kimono (kə mō′nō) a traditional Japanese garment with short, wide sleeves and a sash

❖ She wore a *kimono* made of the finest silk for the special occasion.

dusk (dusk) the time of day when the sun is about to set

❖ The mother worried when her children had not returned by *dusk*.

barren (bar′ən) having no fruit or flowers

❖ The apple trees were *barren*, so the man could not make fresh apple pie.

procession (prō sesh′ən) a group of people moving in an orderly way

❖ The military *procession* passed by slowly.

befallen (bē fôl′ən) happened to

❖ Ill fortune had *befallen* the young boy.

bestowed (bē stōd′) gave or presented as a gift

❖ The princess *bestowed* a kiss upon the frog.

Once upon a time, in a village of Japan, there lived a kind old man and woman with their little dog, Shiro. They called him Shiro because he was as white as snow. Since they had no children, they treated Shiro just like their own child, and took him everywhere they went. When the old man went out into his garden to tend the little dwarfed pine trees, Shiro ran along at his side. When the old man dug up turnips and sweet potatoes from his vegetable garden, Shiro would carry them back to the old woman. He was a very wise dog indeed, and the old man and woman loved him dearly.

One day, as the old man worked in his vegetable plot, Shiro sniffed about in the corners of the garden. Suddenly, he ran to the old man and began to tug at the sleeve of his *kimono*.

"Here, here, Shiro, what are you doing? You'll tear my clothes!" said the old man. But Shiro would not stop. He barked and tugged as hard as he could, until finally the old man decided to see what was the matter. He followed Shiro to a corner of the garden and there Shiro began to scratch the ground and bark, "Wuf-wuf, dig here! Wuf-wuf, dig here!"

"Dig here? In this bare corner, Shiro?" asked the old man.

"Wuf-wuf!" answered Shiro, wagging his tail happily.

"Well, just as you say," said the old man, and he began to dig in the hard, dry soil. Down went the shovel, and up came the dirt! "Heave ho, heave ho. . . . Yoi-sho, yoi-sho!" sang the old man as he dug. Suddenly he heard a clink-clank, clink-clank, as his shovel struck something hard. He looked closely, and to his surprise, he saw hundreds of sparkling gold coins.

"My, my, what is this!" he exclaimed happily, and then he ran home to tell the old woman of the treasure he had discovered. The old woman hurried to the spot with him, and together they filled a large sack full of coins and carried it back to the house.

"We will never be poor again," said the old man happily. "And we owe it all to Shiro!"

"Yes, yes, we would never have discovered the treasure without him," said the old woman.

Then they both stroked Shiro's head tenderly and they gave him a big dinner of rice and fish which he liked so well.

Now there was a very greedy and wicked man who lived next door to the kind old man and woman. When he heard of the treasure which his neighbor had discovered, he quickly ran over to borrow Shiro, for he wanted the dog to do the same thing for him.

He bowed very low and said to the kind old man, "Would you be good enough to let me borrow Shiro for the day?"

"Why, of course," answered the kind old man, for he was a very generous person indeed.

The greedy man took Shiro by the collar and hurried with him out into his own garden.

"Now show me where my treasure is!" he shouted at Shiro, as he dragged him about the garden. But Shiro would do nothing. "Bark quickly and show me the spot, or I will beat you with my shovel," he cried.

Poor little Shiro became so frightened that at last he weakly cried, "Wuf-wuf, dig here." The greedy man then began to dig just as quickly as he could. The shovel went down and the dirt flew up. Suddenly he heard a clink-clank as his shovel struck something hard. "Ah, here is my treasure," said the man greedily, but when he reached down to gather the coins, he found only a mass of dirty rocks and pebbles.

"You have tricked me!" he shouted angrily at Shiro. "And for that you deserve to die!" Then he struck Shiro on the head with his shovel and killed him.

Now, the kind old man knew nothing of all this, so when dusk came and still Shiro had not returned, he decided to go after him. He knocked on the door of his neighbor's house and called, "I've come for Shiro, for it is time for his supper."

The wicked man came to the door and said with a scowl, "Oh, have you come for that worthless dog of yours? He tricked me and gave me rocks instead of coins, so I killed him."

"Oh, my poor little Shiro," cried the kind old man. He ran out to the garden and picked up the body of his little dog. Then he gently carried it home. The old man and woman were very, very sad. They buried Shiro in their garden and planted a little pine tree on his grave. Before long, the little tree grew so large that the old man could no longer put his arms around its trunk.

One day the old woman said, "Let us make something fine and useful from the wood of this pine tree so that we will always have something with which to remember Shiro."

"Ah, a fine idea," agreed the old man. "What shall I make from the wood?"

"I need a new bowl in which to grind rice flour," answered the old woman. "Then I will be able to make some rice cakes, which Shiro liked so well, for our New Year's celebration."

"Then that is what I shall make for you," said the old man, and he cut down the pine tree and made a beautiful big bowl for the old woman. He polished the wood until it gleamed, and then he said, "Now I will help you grind rice flour, and you can make some rice cakes."

Together the old man and woman began to pound and grind the rice in their new bowl. Suddenly they both stopped, for something very strange was happening. The amount of rice in the bowl seemed to be growing and growing, until soon it was overflowing onto the floor. Before they could stop it, the floor was covered with rice, and soon it began to flow out into their yard.

"Just see what is happening!" cried the old woman. "We shall never have to worry about going hungry, for this is enough rice to last us all our lives."

"Indeed it is," said the old man. "Why, this bowl must be filled with magic! Or perhaps Shiro is still helping us!"

The old man and woman had just gathered up all their rice and stored it away carefully when they heard a knock on their door. It was their greedy neighbor who had seen what had happened.

Once again he bowed very politely and asked, "I wonder if I may borrow your lovely new bowl for a day or two?"

"Why, of course you may," answered the generous old man, and so his neighbor carried off the beautiful new rice bowl. Quickly he put in some rice, and began to grind it into flour. "Give me rice! Lots of rice!" he sang out as he ground the rice. He watched the bowl anxiously, waiting for it to overflow with rice, but nothing happened. At last something seemed to bubble up from the bottom of the bowl. The greedy man rubbed his hands together and waited to catch the rice, but instead of rice, dirty rocks and pebbles came tumbling out of the bowl. Soon his house and garden were filled with them. The greedy man shrieked with rage and threw the new bowl onto the hard floor where it broke into many pieces.

"Ah, you worthless wooden bowl!" he shouted, "I will use you for kindling wood!" And he threw the lovely bowl into his stove and set fire to it.

When the kind old man went to get his bowl, his wicked neighbor said, "Oh, have you come for that bowl? It was useless, so I burned it in my stove."

"Oh, but we made that bowl in memory of our dear Shiro," said the kind old man. He felt very sad, but he knew it was useless to argue with his neighbor so he simply asked, "If you cannot give me my bowl, will you at least let me have the ashes that remain from it?"

"Take them, for they are of no use to me," answered the wicked man.

And so the kind old man scooped out the ashes that had fallen beneath the grating of the stove and carried them home in a barrel. As he walked home, with the barrel under his arm, a breeze came along and began to carry the ashes away. They scattered about in the air and fell on the barren branches of the cherry trees that stood along the road. Then something very wonderful happened. As soon as the ashes came to rest on a branch, that branch became covered with beautiful pink blossoms. The old man could scarcely believe his eyes. "It is a miracle! A true miracle!" Then he hurried home to tell the old woman what had happened.

As he told her about the ashes that brought forth lovely cherry blossoms on the barren trees, he had a wonderful idea. "Just think what I could do!" he said to her. "I could go about the countryside covering all the bare trees with beautiful blossoms. How happy everyone would be to see the trees blossoming at this time of year!" The old man chuckled with glee at the thought, and the old woman hastened to make a little red cap and a blue quilted jacket for the old man to wear on his journey.

When all was ready, the old man put on his bright new clothes, strapped the barrel of ashes on his back, and set out on his journey. He walked along the road, scattering ashes on all the trees and singing in a loud, clear voice,

"I will make the flowers bloom,
Old man of the flowers!
On dead branches, flowers gay,
Old man of the flowers!"

He smiled cheerfully, as beautiful flowers blossomed forth on all the dry, brown branches. It seemed just like spring again.

As he walked along, he saw a cloud of dust coming toward him. When it came closer, he could see that it was a long procession of men on horseback. Soon he knew that it was the prince riding back to his palace.

"Well, well, what has happened?" asked the prince looking about. "These trees should not be in bloom in the middle of winter!" Then he saw what the old man was doing, and he heard his little song. "Well, my good man," he called to the kind old man. "You have made the countryside beautiful with your magical ashes, and you will bring much happiness to all my people." Turning to his servant he said, "See that this old man of the flowers is given much food, clothing, and money. He deserves a reward for such a good deed."

"Oh, thank you, sir! Thank you very much," said the old man happily. Then he hurried home to tell the old woman of the wonderful good fortune that had befallen him.

Now when their greedy neighbor heard of the many rewards which the prince had bestowed upon the kind old man, he was even more envious than before. "I too must get a reward from the prince," he said to himself, and he hastily gathered up the ashes that remained in his stove. He too put on a red cap and a blue quilted jacket just as the kind old man had done, and singing the same song, he set out on the road. Soon he saw the prince approaching with his men, so he began to scatter his ashes all about and to sing in a loud voice,

"I will make the flowers bloom,
Old man of the flowers!
On dead branches, flowers gay,
Old man of the flowers!"

But as he threw the ashes, they did not turn into beautiful flowers at all. Instead, they blew right into the eyes and noses of the prince and all his men.

"What is the meaning of this!" shouted the prince angrily. "What do you think you are doing?" he called to the greedy man, as he wiped ashes from his face.

"But sir, I am the old man of the flowers. I was only trying to make the trees blossom again," murmured the greedy neighbor.

"You are not the true old man of the flowers. You are only trying to do as he did, so that you too will be rewarded," retorted the prince. "For being such a greedy and wicked man, you will be punished and sent to jail." As the prince spoke, his servants rushed toward the wicked man and tied him securely so he could not escape.

"Have pity on me! Please let me go!" he cried, but it was of no use.

And so the greedy neighbor was taken away to be punished for his many wicked deeds, while the kind old man and woman lived happily ever after.

READING FOR UNDERSTANDING

1. How do the old man and woman obtain their treasure of gold coins?

2. Why does the neighbor think Shiro tricked him?

3. Why does the old man make a wooden bowl?

4. What happens as the old man scatters the bowl's ashes throughout the countryside?

5. Why does the prince send the neighbor to jail?

RESPONDING TO THE STORY

The old man and woman share their good fortune with others and something good happens to them in return. Has anyone shared something of value with you or with someone you have heard or read about? How did the act of sharing make both the giver and the receiver feel?

REVIEWING VOCABULARY

Fill in each blank with the correct word from the following list: *bestowed, barren, procession, dusk, befallen.*

1. The bridesmaids looked nervous during their _____ down the aisle.

2. How could such bad things have _____ such a wonderful person?

3. Latoya made a wish on the first star that appeared at _____ .

4. The garden was _____ after months of neglect.

5. Ian felt unworthy of the lavish gifts his aunt _____ on him.

THINKING CRITICALLY

1. Why do you think Shiro's magic produced good things for the old couple and bad things for the neighbor?

2. Why do you think the old man is filled with such happiness by being able to bring beautiful flowers to his community?

WRITING PROJECTS

1. Write two more verses for the old man's song. The verses should explain how the old man enjoys sharing with his community.

2. Write another scene for the folktale telling what magical thing happens in the community when the wind blows the blossoms off of the cherry trees.

THE SILENT LOBBY

Mildred Pitts Walter

There are times we, as a community, need to take a stand for what we believe. Together, we may even have to overcome serious obstacles such as discrimination, violence, and repeated setbacks. It takes strength and determination to continue on a course that is blocked by others.

It is the 1960s. African Americans are fighting hard for their civil rights. In this fictional account, when members of the Mississippi Freedom Democratic Party elected to the U.S. House of Representatives are not allowed to take office, a group of African Americans stands up for their rights. With persistence and courage, they travel to Washington, D.C., and refuse to let anything stop them from getting their powerful message all the way to the Capitol.

VOCABULARY WORDS

poll tax (pōl taks) a tax one must pay to vote
❖ The U.S. Constitution prohibits the collecting of a *poll tax* for federal elections.

literacy (lit′ər ə sē) the ability to read and write
❖ Sweden has a high *literacy* rate, so most of its adult population can read.

interpret (in tʉr′prət) to explain the meaning of
❖ She had to *interpret* the article about elections in the United States.

affidavits (af′ə dā′vits) written declarations made under oath before an official
❖ They signed *affidavits* saying that the information they had provided was truthful.

petitions (pə tish′ənz) written documents in which certain rights or benefits are requested or demanded
❖ Many people signed the *petitions* to improve city services.

lobby (läb′ē) to try to affect the decisions of lawmakers
❖ Some people *lobby* to try to affect the decisions of lawmakers.

credentials (kri den′shəlz) evidence that proves a person has certain rights or authority
❖ You need proper *credentials* to get a driver's license.

segregated (seg′rə gāt′id) divided according to ethnicity
❖ In this *segregated* city, each neighborhood is mostly populated by a single ethnic group.

 **T**he old bus chugged along the Mississippi highway toward Washington, D.C. I shivered from icy winds and from excitement and fear. Excitement about going to Washington and fear that the old bus would stall again on the dark, lonely, icy road and we'd never make it.

Oh, just to sleep. The chug-chug-chugging of the old motor was not smooth enough to make soothing sounds, and I could not forget the words Mama and Papa had said just before me and Papa left to pick up twenty other people who filled the bus.

"It's too dangerous," Mama had said. "They just might bomb that bus."

"They could bomb this house for that matter," Papa said.

"I know," Mama went on. "That's why I don't want you to go. Why can't you just forget about this voting business and let us live in peace?"

"There can be no peace without freedom," Papa said.

"And you think someone is going to give you freedom?" Mama asked with heat in her voice. "Instead of going to Washington, you should be getting a gun to protect us."

"There are ways to win a struggle without bombs and guns. I'm going to Washington and Craig is going with me."

"Craig is too young."

"He's eleven. That's old enough to know what this is all about," Papa insisted.

I knew. It had all started two years ago, in 1963. Papa was getting ready to go into town to register to vote. Just as he was leaving, Mr. Clem, Papa's boss, came and warned Papa that he should not try to register.

"I intend to register," Papa said.

"If you do, I'll have to fire you." Mr. Clem drove away in a cloud of dust.

"You ought not go," Mama said, alarmed. "You know that people have been arrested and beaten for going down there."

"I'm going," Papa insisted.

"Let me go with you, Papa." I was scared, too, and wanted to be with him if he needed help.

"No, you stay and look after your mama and the house till I get back."

Day turned to night, and Papa had not returned. Mama paced the floor. Was Papa in jail? Had he been beaten? We waited, afraid. Finally, I said, "Mama, I'll go find him."

"Oh, no!" she cried. Her fear scared me more, and I felt angry because I couldn't do anything.

At last we heard Papa's footsteps. The look on his face let us know right away that something was mighty wrong.

"What happened, Sylvester?" Mama asked.

"I paid the poll tax, passed the literacy test, but I didn't interpret the state constitution the way they wanted. So they wouldn't register me."

Feeling a sense of sad relief, I said, "Now you won't lose your job."

"Oh, but I will. I tried to register."

Even losing his job didn't stop Papa from wanting to vote.

One day he heard about Mrs. Fannie Lou Hamer and the Mississippi Freedom Democratic Party. The Freedom Party registered people without charging a poll tax, without a literacy test, and without people having to tell what the Mississippi Constitution was about.

On election day in 1964, Papa proudly voted for Mrs. Hamer, Mrs. Victoria Grey, and Mrs. Annie Devine to represent the people of the Second Congressional

District of Mississippi. Eighty-three thousand other black men and women voted that day, too. Great victory celebrations were held in homes and churches. But the Governor of Mississippi, Paul B. Johnson, declared all of those eighty-three thousand votes of black people illegal. He gave certificates of election to three white men—William Colmer, John Williams, and a Mr. Whittier—to represent the mostly black Second Congressional District.

Members of the Freedom Party were like Papa—they didn't give up. They got busy when the governor threw out their votes. Lawyers from all over the country came to help. People signed affidavits saying that when they tried to register they lost their jobs, they were beaten, and their homes were burned and churches bombed. More than ten thousand people signed petitions to the governor asking him to count their votes. There was never a word from the governor.

My mind returned to the sound of the old bus slowly grinding along. Suddenly the bus stopped. Not again! We'd never make it now. Papa got out in the cold wind and icy drizzling rain and raised the hood. While he worked, we sang and clapped our hands to keep warm. I could hear Sister Phyllis praying with all her might for our safety. After a while we were moving along again.

I must have finally fallen asleep, for a policeman's voice woke me. "You can't stop here near the Capitol," he shouted.

"Our bus won't go, " Papa said

"If you made it from Mississippi all the way to D.C., you'll make it from here," the policeman barked.

At first the loud voice frightened me. Then, wide awake, sensing the policeman's impatience, I wondered why Papa didn't let him know that we would go as soon as the motor started. But Papa, knowing that old bus, said nothing. He stepped on the starter. The old motor growled and died. Again the policeman shouted, "I said get out of here."

"We'll have to push it," Papa said.

Everyone got off the bus and pushed. Passersby stopped and stared. Finally we were safe on a side street, away from the Capitol with a crowd gathered around us.

"You mean they came all the way from Mississippi in that?" someone in the crowd asked.

Suddenly the old bus looked shabby. I lowered my head and became aware of my clothes: my faded coat too small; my cotton pants too thin. With a feeling of shame, I wished those people would go away.

"What brings you all to the District?" a man called to us.

"We've come to see about seating the people we voted for and elected," Papa answered. "Down home they say our votes don't count, and up here they've gone ahead and seated men who don't represent us. We've come to talk about that."

"So you've come to lobby," a woman shouted. The crowd laughed.

Why were they laughing? I knew that to lobby meant to try to get someone to decide for or against something. Yes, that was why we had come. I wished I could have said to those people who stood gawking at us that the suffering that brought us here was surely nothing to laugh about.

The laughter from the crowd quieted when another woman shouted, "You're too late to lobby. The House of Representatives will vote on that issue this morning."

Too late. That's what had worried me when the old bus kept breaking down. Had we come so far in this cold for nothing? Was it really too late to talk to members of the House of Representatives to persuade them to seat our representatives elected by the Freedom

Party, *not* the ones chosen by the governor?

Just then rain began to fall. The crowd quickly left, and we climbed onto our bus. Papa and the others started to talk. What would we do now? Finally Papa said, "We can't turn back now. We've done too much and come too far."

After more talk we all agreed that we must try to do what we had come to do. Icy rain pelted us as we rushed against cold wind back to the Capitol.

A doorman stopped us on the steps. "May I have your passes?"

"We don't have any," Papa replied.

"Sorry, you have to have passes for seats in the gallery." The doorman blocked the way.

"We're cold in this rain. Let us in," Sister Phyllis cried.

"Maybe we should just go on back home," someone suggested.

"Yes. We can't talk to the legislators now, anyway," another woman said impatiently.

"No," Papa said. "We must stay if we do no more than let them see that we have come all this way."

"But we're getting soaking wet. We can't stand out here much longer," another protested.

"Can't you just let us in out of this cold?" Papa pleaded with the doorman.

"Not without passes." The doorman still blocked the way. Then he said, "There's a tunnel underneath this building. You can go there to get out of the rain."

We crowded into the tunnel and lined up along the sides. My chilled body and hands came to life pressed against the warm walls. Then footsteps and voices echoed through the tunnel. Police. This tunnel . . . a trap! Would they do something to us for trying to get in without passes? I wanted to cry out to Papa, but I could not speak.

The footsteps came closer. Then many people began to walk by. When they came upon us, they suddenly stopped talking. Only the sound of their feet echoed in the tunnel. Where had they come from? What did they do? "Who are they, Papa?" I whispered.

"Congressmen and women." Papa spoke so softly, I hardly heard him, even in the silence.

They wore warm coats, some trimmed with fur. Their shoes gleamed. Some of them frowned at us. Others glared. Some sighed quickly as they walked by. Others looked at us, then turned their eyes to their shoes. I could tell by a sudden lift of the head and a certain look that some were surprised and scared. And there were a few whose friendly smiles seemed to say, Right on!

I glanced at Papa. How poor he and our friends looked beside those well-dressed people. Their clothes were damp, threadbare, and wrinkled; their shoes were worn and mud stained. But they all stood straight and tall.

My heart pounded. I wanted to call out to those men and women, "Count my papa's vote! Let my people help make laws, too." But I didn't dare speak in that silence.

Could they hear my heart beating? Did they know what was on my mind? "Lord," I prayed, "let them hear us in this silence."

Then two congressmen stopped in front of Papa. I was frightened until I saw smiles on their faces.

"I'm Congressman Ryan from New York," one of them said. Then he introduced a black man: "This is Congressman Hawkins from California."

"I'm Sylvester Saunders. We are here from Mississippi," Papa said.

"We expected you much earlier," Congressman Ryan said.

"Our old bus and bad weather delayed us," Papa explained.

"That's unfortunate. You could've helped us a lot. We worked late into the night lobbying to get votes on your side. But maybe I should say on *our* side." Mr. Ryan smiled.

"And we didn't do very well," Congressman Hawkins said.

"We'll be lucky if we get fifty votes on our side today," Congressman Ryan informed us. "Maybe you would like to come in and see us at work."

"We don't have passes," I said, surprised at my voice.

"We'll see about getting all of you in," Congressman Hawkins promised.

A little later, as we found seats in the gallery, Congressman Gerald Ford from the state of Michigan was speaking. He did not want Mrs. Hamer and other fairly elected members of the Freedom Party seated in the House. He asked his fellow congressmen to stick to the rule of letting only those with credentials from their states be seated in Congress. The new civil rights act would, in time, undo wrongs done to black Americans. But for now, Congress should let the men chosen by Governor Johnson keep their seats and get on with other business.

Then Congressman Ryan rose to speak. How could Congress stick to rules that denied blacks their right to vote in the state of Mississippi? The rule of letting only those with credentials from a segregated state have seats in the House could not *justly* apply here.

I looked down on those men and few women and wondered if they were listening. Did they know about the petitions? I remembered what Congressman Ryan had said: "We'll be lucky if we get fifty. . . ." Only 50 out of 435 elected to the House.

Finally the time came for Congress to vote. Those who wanted to seat Mrs. Hamer and members of the

Freedom Democratic Party were to say, yes. Those who didn't want to seat Mrs. Hamer were to say, no.

At every yes vote I could hardly keep from clapping my hands and shouting, "Yea! Yea!" But I kept quiet, counting: thirty, then forty, forty-eight .... only two more. We would lose badly.

Then something strange happened. Congressmen and congresswomen kept saying "Yes. Yes. Yes." On and on, "Yes." My heart pounded. Could we win? I sat on my hands to keep from clapping. I looked at Papa and the others who had come with us. They all sat on the edge of their seats. They looked as if they could hardly keep from shouting out, too, as more yes votes rang from the floor.

When the voting was over, 148 votes had been cast in our favor. What had happened? Why had so many changed their minds?

Later, Papa introduced me to Congressman Hawkins. The congressman asked me, "How did you all know that some of us walk through that tunnel from our offices?"

"We didn't know," I answered. "We were sent there out of the rain."

"That's strange," the congressman said. "Your standing there silently made a difference in the vote. Even though we lost this time, some of them now know that we'll keep on lobbying until we win."

I felt proud. Papa had been right when he said to Mama, "There are ways to win a struggle without bombs and guns." We had lobbied in silence and we had been *heard*.

READING FOR UNDERSTANDING

1. Why does Mama not want Papa to register to vote?

2. Why is Papa not allowed to register to vote?

3. How do members of the Freedom Party respond when their candidates are not allowed to take office?

4. Why does the group from Mississippi wait in the tunnel?

5. What happens during the vote in Congress?

RESPONDING TO THE STORY

Even though Craig was not old enough to vote, he understood the importance of what his father was fighting for and that the outcome of their efforts would one day affect his own life. Write a paragraph explaining how you would feel and what you would do if your right to vote were threatened. Would you have the courage to stand up for your rights?

REVIEWING VOCABULARY

Match each word on the left with the correct definition on the right.

1. affidavits   **a.** evidence that proves a person has certain rights or authority

2. segregated   **b.** to try to affect the decisions of lawmakers

3. credentials   **c.** written declarations made under oath

4. petitions   **d.** divided according to ethnicity

5. lobby   **e.** written documents in which rights or benefits are requested or demanded

THINKING CRITICALLY

1. Why do you think Craig's father wants his son to come to Washington with the group of adults?

2. What other types of situations might require people to show the same kind of determination that Craig's father and members of the Mississippi Freedom Democratic Party showed?

WRITING PROJECTS

1. Write a newspaper article covering one of the important events that takes place in this story. You may wish to consider the words and actions of the people in your story, and how they were able to overcome any difficulties they may have experienced.

2. Write another scene for the story that describes the way the characters feel and what they say during the ride back to Mississippi.

THE GENTLEMAN OF RÍO EN MEDIO

Juan Sedillo

Think about a neighborhood park where you and your family and friends like to spend time. The park belongs to the city, but in many ways it also belongs to the people who enjoy it—you and your community.

In this story, Don Anselmo of Río en Medio sells some land. The new owners are soon complaining that the village children continue to play in the orchard on the property. Read this story to find out a new way to look at the idea of ownership.

VOCABULARY WORDS

negotiations (ni gō´shē ā´shənz) discussions to get different groups to agree on an issue

❖ She signed her new contract after a long series of *negotiations*.

tilled (tild) prepared land to raise crops on it

❖ In order to prepare for the new growing season, the farmer *tilled* her fields.

innumerable (in no͞o´mer ə bəl) very many; too numerous to be counted

❖ The *innumerable* coins filled chest after chest to the brim.

kin (kin) family members; relatives

❖ I met *kin* I never knew I had at last year's family reunion.

survey (sər vā´) to determine the boundaries of a piece of land

❖ Malcolm hired two people to *survey* his land so he'd know exactly where to build his fence.

deed (dēd) a document that proves ownership of property

❖ When she sold the house, she gave up the *deed*.

broached (brōcht) brought up for discussion

❖ He *broached* the topic of how to spend their vacation to the whole family.

descendants (dē sen´dənt) people who are the offspring of a certain ancestor, family, or group

❖ We are *descendants* of a pioneer family who left Virginia to settle in Oregon.

It took months of negotiations to come to an understanding with the old man. He was in no hurry. What he had the most of was time. He lived up in Río en Medio, where his people had been for hundreds of years. He tilled the same land they had tilled. His house was small and wretched, but quaint. The little creek ran through his land. His orchard was gnarled and beautiful.

The day of the sale he came into the office. His coat was old, green, and faded. I thought of Senator Catron, who had been such a power with these people up there in the mountains. Perhaps it was one of his old Prince Alberts. He also wore gloves. They were old and torn and his fingertips showed through them. He carried a cane, but it was only the skeleton of a worn-out umbrella. Behind him walked one of his innumerable kin—a dark young man with eyes like a gazelle.

The old man bowed to all of us in the room. Then he removed his hat and gloves, slowly and carefully. Chaplin once did that in a picture, in a bank—he was the janitor. Then he handed his things to the boy, who stood obediently behind the old man's chair.

There was a great deal of conversation, about rain and about his family. He was very proud of his large family. Finally we got down to business. Yes, he would sell, as he had agreed, for twelve hundred dollars, in cash. We would buy, and the money was ready. "Don Anselmo," I said to him in Spanish, "we have made a discovery. You remember that we sent that surveyor, that engineer, up there to survey your land so as to make the deed. Well, he finds that you own more than eight acres. He tells us that your land extends across the river and that you own almost twice as much as you thought." He didn't know that. "And now, Don Anselmo," I added, "these Americans are *buena gente*, they are good people, and they are willing to pay you for the additional land as well, at the same rate per acre, so that instead of twelve hundred dollars you will get almost twice as much, and the money is here for you."

The old man hung his head for a moment in thought. Then he stood up and stared at me. "Friend," he said, "I do not like to have you speak to me in that manner." I kept still and let him have his say. "I know these Americans are good people, and that is why I have agreed to sell my house to them. But I do not care to be insulted. I have agreed to sell my house and land for twelve hundred dollars and that is the price."

I argued with him but it was useless. Finally he signed the deed and took the money but refused to take more than the amount agreed upon. Then he shook hands all around, put on his ragged gloves, took his stick and walked out with the boy behind him.

A month later my friends had moved into Río en Medio. They had replastered the old adobe house, pruned the trees, patched the fence, and moved in for the summer. One day they came back to the office to complain. The children of the village were overrunning their property. They came every day and played under the trees, built little play fences around them, and took blossoms. When they were spoken to they only laughed and talked back good-naturedly in Spanish.

I sent a messenger up to the mountains for Don Anselmo. It took a week to arrange another meeting. When he arrived he repeated his previous preliminary performance. He wore the same faded cutaway, carried the same stick, and was accompanied by the boy again. He shook hands all around, sat down with the boy behind his chair, and talked about the weather. Finally I broached the subject. "Don Anselmo, about the ranch you sold to these people. They are good people and want to be your friends and neighbors always. When you sold to them you signed a document, a deed, and in that deed you agreed to several things. One thing was that they were to have the complete possession of the property. Now, Don Anselmo, it seems that every day the children of the village overrun the orchard and spend most of their time there. We would like to know if you, as the most respected man in the village, could not stop them from doing so in order that these people may enjoy their new home more in peace."

Don Anselmo stood up. "We have all learned to love these Americans," he said, "because they are good people and good neighbors. I sold them my property because I knew they were good people, but I did not sell them the trees in the orchard."

This was bad. "Don Anselmo," I pleaded, "when one signs a deed and sells real property one sells also everything that grows on the land, and those trees, every one of them, are on the land and inside the boundaries of what you sold."

"Yes, I admit that," he said. "You know," he added, "I am the oldest man in the village. Almost everyone there is my relative and all the children of Río en Medio are my *sobrinos* and *nietos*, my descendants. Every time a child has been born in Río en Medio since I took possession of that house from my mother, I have planted a tree for that child. The trees in the orchard are not mine, *Señor*, they belong to the children of the village. Every person in Río en Medio born since the railroad came to Santa Fe owns a tree in that orchard. I did not sell the trees because I could not. They are not mine."

There was nothing we could do. Legally we owned the trees, but the old man had been so generous, refusing what amounted to a fortune for him. It took most of the following winter to buy the trees, individually, from the descendants of Don Anselmo in the valley of Río en Medio.

READING FOR UNDERSTANDING

1. Who is telling the story?

2. What is most important to Don Anselmo?

3. What is most important to the Americans?

4. During meetings with the narrator, what does Don Anselmo talk about before he will discuss the issue that brought him there?

5. In what two very different ways does the community benefit from Don Anselmo's gift?

RESPONDING TO THE STORY

Don Anselmo gives to his community by planting an orchard that he believes truly belongs to the villagers. Describe other ways in which people can take pride in and contribute to their community.

REVIEWING VOCABULARY

Fill in each blank with the correct word from the following list: *negotiations, survey, broached, descendants, innumerable.*

1. To measure exactly how big ten acres is, we'll have to _____ the land.

2. Out in the country, we had a better view of the _____ stars.

3. Joaquin nervously _____ the subject of marriage to his girlfriend.

4. Chang's father and uncle are _____ of famous Chinese warriors.

5. The _____ went poorly, and the president stormed out of the company meeting.

THINKING CRITICALLY

1. Why do you think Don Anselmo won't take any more money for the additional acres the surveyor found?

2. Why does Don Anselmo say that the trees belong to the villagers?

WRITING PROJECTS

1. Imagine that you are one of Don Anselmo's descendants. Write a paragraph describing your feelings about the trees he has planted.

2. Write a travel brochure that tourists would read when visiting your community. Include a brief history of the area and descriptions of the aspects of your community of which you are most proud.

DIARY OF A YOUNG GIRL
by Anne Frank

How do you maintain your values, goals, and principles when your entire world changes for the worse? This is a question that Anne Frank may have asked herself during the time that her family and the van Daan family are hiding in the Annex, a secret room behind her father's store. It is 1942 in the Netherlands, and the German Nazis are rounding up European Jews and sending them to almost certain death in the concentration camps. The Franks and the van Daans are Jewish.

For more than two years, these two families live together in a few cramped rooms, hiding from the Nazis. Anne, 13 years old at the time they flee to the Annex, records her thoughts and feelings in her diary. Despite the incredible difficulties that she faces every day and her uncertain future, young Anne maintains a love for life and a sense of hope well beyond her years.

VOCABULARY WORDS

bare (ber) to expose; to open to view
❖ Wolves growl and *bare* their teeth to show anger.

biased (bī´əst) prejudiced; leaning toward a certain opinion
❖ The mother was *biased* in her judgment of which child sang best.

adage (ad´ij) an old saying that has been popularly accepted as a truth
❖ My uncle includes at least one *adage* in every conversation.

curb (kʉrb) to control or restrain
❖ The boy does not seem to want to *curb* his outbursts.

alienated (āl´yən āt id) removed; withdrawn
❖ Lucy introduced herself to the new student so he wouldn't feel *alienated* on his first day.

egotistical (ē´gō tis´ti kəl) selfish; self-absorbed
❖ *Egotistical* people often fail to think about others.

intimacy (in´tə mə sē) closeness; very strong friendship
❖ *Intimacy* between friends often grows with time.

predominates (prē däm´ə nāts) is dominant in amount or number
❖ In an uncomfortable situation, a feeling of anxiety often *predominates*.

Saturday, July 15, 1944

Dearest Kitty,

We've received a book from the library with the challenging title *What Do You Think of the Modern Young Girl?* I'd like to discuss this subject today.

The writer criticizes "today's youth" from head to toe, though without dismissing them all as "hopeless cases." On the contrary, she believes they have it within their power to build a bigger, better, and more beautiful world, but that they occupy themselves with superficial things, without giving a thought to true beauty.

In some passages I had the strong feeling that the writer was directing her disapproval at me, which is why I finally want to bare my soul to you and defend myself against this attack.

I have one outstanding character trait that must be obvious to anyone who's known me for any length of time: I have a great deal of self-knowledge. In everything I do, I can watch myself as if I were a stranger. I can stand across from the everyday Anne and, without being biased or making excuses, watch what she's doing, both the good and the bad. This self-awareness never leaves me, and every time I open my mouth, I think, "You should have said that differently" or "That's fine the way it is." I condemn myself in so many ways that I'm beginning to realize the truth of Father's adage: "Every child has to raise itself." Parents can only advise their children or point them in the right direction. Ultimately, people shape their own characters. In addition, I face life with an extraordinary amount of courage. I feel so strong and capable of bearing burdens, so young and free! When I first realized this, I was glad, because it means I can more easily withstand the blows life has in store.

But I've talked about these things so often. Now I'd like to turn to the chapter "Father and Mother Don't Understand Me." My parents have always spoiled me rotten, treated me kindly, defended me against the van Daans and done all that parents can. And yet for the longest time I've felt extremely lonely, left out, neglected and misunderstood. Father did everything he could to curb my rebellious spirit, but it was no use. I've cured myself by holding my behavior up to the light and looking at what I was doing wrong.

Why didn't Father support me in my struggle? Why did he fall short when he tried to offer me a helping hand? The answer is: He used the wrong methods. He always talked to me as if I were a child going through a difficult phase. It sounds crazy, since Father's the only one who's given me a sense of confidence and made me feel as if I'm a sensible person. But he overlooked one thing: He failed to see that this struggle to triumph over my difficulties was more important to me than anything else. I didn't want to hear about "typical adolescent problems," or "other girls," or "you'll grow out of it." I didn't want to be treated the same as all-the-other-girls, but as Anne-in-her-own-right, and Pim didn't understand that. Besides, I can't confide in anyone unless they tell me a lot about themselves, and because I know very little about him, I can't get on a more intimate footing. Pim always acts like the elderly father who once had the same fleeting impulses, but who can no longer relate to me as a friend, no matter how hard he tries. As a result, I've never shared my outlook on life or my long-pondered theories with anyone but my diary and, once in a while, Margot. I've hid anything having to do with me from Father, never shared my ideals with him, deliberately alienated myself from him.

I couldn't have done it any other way. I've let myself be guided entirely by my feelings. It was egotistical, but I've done what was best for my own peace of mind. I would lose that, plus the self-confidence I've worked so hard to achieve, if I were to be subjected to criticism halfway through the job. It may sound hard-hearted, but I can't take criticism from Pim either, because not only do I never share my innermost thoughts with him, but I've pushed him even further away by being irritable.

This is a point I think about quite often: Why is it that Pim annoys me so much sometimes? I can hardly bear to have him tutor me, and his affection seems forced. I want to be left alone, and I'd rather he ignored me for a while until I'm more sure of myself when I'm talking to him! I'm still torn with guilt about the mean letter I wrote him when I was so upset. Oh, it's hard to be strong and brave in every way!

Still, this hasn't been my greatest disappointment. No, I think about Peter much more than I do Father. I know very well that he was my conquest, and not the other way around. I created an image of him in my mind, pictured him as a quiet, sweet, sensitive boy badly in need of friendship and love! I needed to pour out my heart to a living person. I wanted a friend who would help me find my way again. I accomplished what I set out to do and drew him, slowly but surely, toward me. When I finally got him to be my friend, it automatically developed into an intimacy that, when I think about it now, seems outrageous. We talked about the most private things, but we haven't yet touched upon the things closest to my heart. I still can't make head or tail of Peter. Is he superficial, or is it shyness that holds him back, even with me? But putting all that aside, I made one mistake: I used intimacy to get closer to him, and in doing so, I ruled out other forms of friendship.

He longs to be loved, and I can see he's beginning to like me more with each passing day. Our time together leaves him feeling satisfied, but just makes me want to start all over again. I never broach the subjects I long to bring out in the open. I forced Peter, more than he realizes, to get close to me, and now he's holding on for dear life. I honestly don't see any effective way of shaking him off and getting him back on his own two feet. I soon realized he could never be a kindred spirit, but still tried to help him break out of his narrow world and expand his youthful horizons.

"Deep down, the young are lonelier than the old." I read this in a book somewhere and it's stuck in my mind. As far as I can tell, it's true.

So if you're wondering whether it's harder for the adults here than for the children, the answer is no, it's certainly not. Older people have an opinion about everything and are sure of themselves and their actions. It's twice as hard for us young people to hold on to our opinions at a time when ideals are being shattered and destroyed, when the worst side of human nature predominates, when everyone has come to doubt truth, justice, and God.

Anyone who claims that the older folks have a more difficult time in the Annex doesn't realize that the problems have a far greater impact on *us*. We're much too young to deal with these problems, but they keep thrusting themselves on us until, finally, we're forced to think up a solution, though most of the time our solutions crumble when faced with the facts. It's difficult in times like these: Ideals, dreams and cherished hopes rise within us, only to be crushed by grim reality. It's a wonder I haven't abandoned all my ideals; they seem so absurd and impractical. Yet I cling to them because I still believe, in spite of everything, that people are truly good at heart.

It's utterly impossible for me to build my life on a foundation of chaos, suffering and death. I see the world being slowly transformed into a wilderness, I hear the approaching thunder that, one day, will destroy us too, I feel the suffering of millions. And yet, when I look up at the sky, I somehow feel that everything will change for the better, that this cruelty too shall end, that peace and tranquility will return once more. In the meantime, I must hold on to my ideals. Perhaps the day will come when I'll be able to realize them!

Yours, Anne M. Frank

READING FOR UNDERSTANDING

1. What does Anne feel her most obvious character trait is?

2. Why does Anne come to believe that her father was correct when he said, "Every child has to raise itself"?

3. Why did Anne seek Peter's friendship?

4. What is the "grim reality" that Anne refers to toward the end of her diary entry?

5. What are Anne's hopes for the future?

RESPONDING TO THE STORY

In this section from her diary, Anne Frank reflects on the problems that she has growing up. She also holds on to her belief in a better future. Do you think that you would be able to keep a positive attitude if faced with Anne's situation? Explain your answer.

REVIEWING VOCABULARY

1. The woman ended her speech with an *adage*, or **(a)** well-known poem **(b)** humorous story **(c)** popular saying.

2. After a natural disaster, chaos often *predominates*; in other words, there is **(a)** an almost equal amount of chaos and order **(b)** more chaos than order **(c)** less chaos than order.

3. An *intimacy* had gradually developed between the two; now they **(a)** were fiercely competitive **(b)** were very close friends **(c)** rarely communicated.

4. An *alienated* person may feel **(a)** popular **(b)** busy **(c)** lonely.

5. Eugene was so *egotistical* that he usually thought only about **(a)** his parents **(b)** himself **(c)** others.

THINKING CRITICALLY

1. Why does Anne believe she can "more easily withstand the blows life has in store"?

2. Anne feels that the situation her family and the van Daan family are facing is harder for the children to deal with than it is for the adults. Why do you think she feels this way?

WRITING PROJECTS

1. Write a journal entry about an issue that you think concerns the youth of today.

2. Write a paragraph responding to the part in Anne's diary where she writes: "I still believe, in spite of everything, that people are truly good at heart."

"Our task must be to free ourselves . . . by widening our circle of compassion to embrace all living creatures and the whole of nature and its beauty." — Albert Einstein

Unit 4

CARETAKERS OF THE EARTH

THE SPARROW
by Ivan Turgenev

Everyday, all around us, we see parents protect and care for their children. Stories of parents facing dangerous situations to save their children are not unusual. They do so out of love. Have you ever wondered if wild animals share these same feelings of love?

In this story, a mother sparrow throws itself in front of a dangerous enemy in an attempt to save her baby. The narrator reacts to the sparrow's action with surprise and wonder. Would you react the same way? Read the story to find out.

VOCABULARY WORDS

stealthily (stel´th ə lē) moving in a secretive way
❖ The robber *stealthily* approached the window so that no one would see or hear him.

misshapen (mis shāp´ən) shaped badly; deformed
❖ The plastic bowl was *misshapen* from the heat of the oven.

frenzied (fren´zēd) wildly excited; frantic
❖ Afraid she was going to be late for class, Lindsay made a *frenzied* search for her books.

perch (pᵾrch) a tree branch on which a bird rests
❖ The bird's *perch* was high in the tree.

hurl (hᵾrl) to throw with force
❖ The baseball player started to *hurl* the ball to first base.

sustained (sə stānd´) kept in existence
❖ The love of his family *sustained* him during his illness.

hastened (hās´ənd) hurried
❖ Andrés was hungry after rehearsal, so he *hastened* home for dinner.

**I** was returning from a day's hunting and was walking toward the house along the alley in my garden. My dog was running ahead of me. Suddenly she slowed her pace and began to advance stealthily, as though she had caught the scent of game.

I looked down the path and saw a young sparrow with a streak of yellow near its beak and a bit of puff on its head. It had fallen out of the nest. (A strong wind was swaying the birch trees.) The tiny bird sat there trying helplessly to use its barely grown wings.

My dog was stealing up to the infant sparrow when, abruptly, an old black-chested bird fell like a stone right in front of the dog's face, and with all its feathers standing on end, misshapen, uttering a desperate and pitiful chirp, it hopped once and then again in the direction of the dog's open jaw.

The bird had thrown itself in front of the dog to shield its young one, but its own small body was trembling with terror, its little voice was frenzied and hoarse, and it was numb with fright—it was sacrificing itself!

What a huge monster the dog must have seemed to the mother sparrow! Nevertheless, it could not bear to stay on its high, safe perch in the tree. A force stronger than its will to remain alive made it hurl itself to the rescue.

My Treasure, the dog, stopped still and then backed up. Evidently she, too, recognized that force. . . .

I hastened to call off the puzzled dog and went on my way, awed.

Yes, do not laugh. I was awed by that small, heroic bird—by its impulse of love.

Love, I felt more than ever, is stronger than death and the fear of death. Only through love is life sustained and nourished.

READING FOR UNDERSTANDING

1. Why isn't the baby sparrow in its nest?

2. How does the dog react to the baby bird?

3. How does the mother bird protect the baby bird?

4. According to the narrator, why does the mother bird want to protect the baby bird?

5. To what conclusion do the mother sparrow's actions lead the narrator?

RESPONDING TO THE STORY

The mother sparrow willingly risks her own life to protect her baby. Describe another way that you or someone you know or have read about demonstrated their love for another person or animal.

REVIEWING VOCABULARY

Fill in each blank with the correct word from the following list: *perch, hurl, frenzied, sustained, hastened.*

1. The owl watched us from its _____ in the tree.

2. Lucinda felt _____ as she rushed to finish her homework.

3. He _____ to answer the ringing doorbell.

4. Kevin tried to _____ the stick over the fence.

5. The babysitter's care and attention _____ the children while their parents were on vacation.

THINKING CRITICALLY

1. The narrator says, "Yes, do not laugh" to the reader when he admits being awed by the mother sparrow's deed. Why do you think he was afraid the reader would laugh at him?

2. Turgenev writes, "A force stronger than its will to remain alive made it hurl itself to the rescue." He believes that force is love. Do you agree? Explain your answer.

WRITING PROJECTS

1. Imagine that the animals in the story can talk. Write a dialogue that might take place between the mother bird and the dog.

2. Write a journal entry responding to Turgenev's statement that life is sustained and nourished only through love.

WE ARE ALL ONE
by Laurence Yep

Would you ever think twice about killing an ant? Many people believe that all life is connected and that what affects one living thing affects all other living things.

In this Chinese legend, a rich man is suffering greatly from an eye disease. He offers a reward to anyone who can cure him. A poor, kind, old peddler goes into the forest outside the city to seek a cure. The peddler believes that "we are all one," and he extends this belief to the creatures he encounters in the forest. Along his way, he performs acts of kindness for them with no thought of their helping him in return. He is therefore surprised by the manner in which he finds the cure.

VOCABULARY WORDS

larvae (lär´vē´) early, immature forms of any animal that changes in structure when it reaches an adult stage
❖ The insect *larvae* covered the mulberry leaf.

escort (es´kôrt´) someone or something that accompanies another for protection
❖ The *escort* of soldiers surrounded the queen in order to protect her.

lacquer (lak´ər) a hard, smooth, shiny varnish
❖ The bookshelf has a *lacquer* finish.

omen (ō´mən) a thing or happening believed to foretell the future
❖ The woman saw the storm as a bad *omen*.

tufts (tufts) bunches of hairs, feathers, grass, etc., growing closely together
❖ The children looked for insects in the *tufts* of grass.

**L**ong ago there was a rich man with a disease in his eyes. For many years, the pain was so great that he could not sleep at night. He saw every doctor he could, but none of them could help him.

"What good is all my money?" he groaned. Finally, he became so desperate that he sent criers through the city offering a reward to anyone who could cure him.

Now in that city lived an old candy peddler. He would walk around with his baskets of candy, but he was so kind-hearted that he gave away as much as he sold, so he was always poor.

When the old peddler heard the announcement, he remembered something his mother had said. She had once told him about a magical herb that was good for the eyes. So he packed up his baskets and went back to the single tiny room in which his family lived.

When he told his plan to his wife, she scolded him, "If you go off on this crazy hunt, how are we supposed to eat?"

Usually the peddler gave in to his wife, but this time he was stubborn. "There are two baskets of candy," he said. "I'll be back before they're gone."

The next morning, as soon as the soldiers opened the gates, he was the first one to leave the city. He did not stop until he was deep inside the woods. As a boy, he had often wandered there. He had liked to pretend that the shadowy forest was a green sea and he was a fish slipping through the cool waters.

As he examined the ground, he noticed ants scurrying about. On their backs were larvae-like, white grains of rice. A rock had fallen into a stream, so the water now spilled into the ants' nest.

"We're all one," the kindhearted peddler said. So he

waded into the shallow stream and put the rock on the bank. Then with a sharp stick, he dug a shallow ditch that sent the rest of the water back into the stream.

Without another thought about his good deed, he began to search through the forest. He looked everywhere; but as the day went on, he grew sleepy. "Ho-hum. I got up too early. I'll just take a short nap," he decided, and lay down in the shade of an old tree, where he fell right asleep.

In his dreams, the old peddler found himself standing in the middle of a great city. Tall buildings rose high overhead. He couldn't see the sky even when he tilted back his head. An escort of soldiers marched up to him with a loud clatter of their black lacquer armor. "Our queen wishes to see you," the captain said.

The frightened peddler could only obey and let the fierce soldiers lead him into a shining palace. There, a woman with a high crown sat upon a tall throne. Trembling, the old peddler fell to his knees and touched his forehead against the floor.

But the queen ordered him to stand. "Like the great Emperor Yü of long ago, you tamed the great flood. We are all one now. You have only to ask, and I or any of my people will come to your aid."

The old peddler cleared his throat. "I am looking for a certain herb. It will cure any disease of the eyes."

The queen shook her head regretfully. "I have never heard of that herb. But you will surely find it if you keep looking for it."

And then the old peddler woke. Sitting up, he saw that in his wanderings he had come back to the ants' nest. It was there he had taken his nap. His dream city had been the ants' nest itself.

"This is a good omen," he said to himself, and he began searching even harder. He was so determined to find the herb that he did not notice how time had passed. He was surprised when he saw how the light was fading. He looked all around then. There was no sight of his city—only strange hills. He realized then that he had searched so far he had gotten lost.

Night was coming fast and with it the cold. He rubbed his arms and hunted for shelter. In the twilight, he thought he could see the green tiles of a roof.

He stumbled through the growing darkness until he reached a ruined temple. Weeds grew through cracks in the stones and most of the roof itself had fallen in. Still, the ruins would provide some protection.

As he started inside, he saw a centipede with bright orange skin and red tufts of fur along its back. Yellow dots covered its sides like a dozen tiny eyes. It was also rushing into the temple as fast as it could, but there was a bird swooping down toward it.

The old peddler waved his arms and shouted, scaring the bird away. Then he put down his palm in front of the insect. "We are all one, you and I." The many feet tickled his skin as the centipede climbed onto his hand.

Inside the temple, he gathered dried leaves and found old sticks of wood, and soon he had a fire going. The peddler even picked some fresh leaves for the centipede from a bush near the temple doorway. "I may have to go hungry, but you don't have to, friend."

Stretching out beside the fire, the old peddler pillowed his head on his arms. He was so tired that he soon fell asleep, but even in his sleep he dreamed he was still searching in the woods. Suddenly he thought he heard footsteps near his head. He woke instantly and looked about, but he only saw the brightly colored centipede.

"Was it you, friend?" The old peddler chuckled and, lying down, he closed his eyes again. "I must be getting nervous."

"We are one, you and I," a voice said faintly—as if from a long distance. "If you go south, you will find a pine tree with two trunks. By its roots, you will find a magic bead. A cousin of mine spat on it years ago. Dissolve that bead in wine and tell the rich man to drink it if he wants to heal his eyes."

The old peddler trembled when he heard the voice because he realized that the centipede was magical. He wanted to run from the temple, but he couldn't even get up. It was if he were glued to the floor.

But then the old peddler reasoned with himself: If the centipede had wanted to hurt me, it could have long ago. Instead, it seems to want to help me.

So the old peddler stayed where he was, but he did not dare open his eyes. When the first sunlight fell through the roof, he raised one eyelid cautiously. There was no sign of the centipede. He sat up and looked around, but the magical centipede was gone.

He followed the centipede's instructions when he left the temple. Traveling south, he kept a sharp eye out for the pine tree with two trunks. He walked until late in the afternoon, but all he saw were normal pine trees.

Wearily he sat down and sighed. Even if he found the pine tree, he couldn't be sure that he would find the bead. Someone else might even have discovered it a long time ago.

But something made him look a little longer. Just when he was thinking about turning back, he saw the odd tree. Somehow his tired legs managed to carry him over to the tree, and he got down on his knees. But the ground was covered with pine needles and his old eyes were too weak. The old peddler could have wept with frustration, and then he remembered the ants.

He began to call, "Ants, ants, we are all one."

Almost immediately, thousands of ants came boiling out of nowhere. Delighted, the old man held up his fingers. "I'm looking for a bead. It might be very tiny."

Then, careful not to crush any of his little helpers, the old man sat down to wait. In no time, the ants reappeared with a tiny bead. With trembling fingers, the old man took the bead from them and examined it. It was colored orange and looked as if it had yellow eyes on the sides.

There was nothing very special about the bead, but the old peddler treated it like a fine jewel. Putting the bead into his pouch, the old peddler bowed his head.

"I thank you and I thank your queen," the old man said. After the ants disappeared among the pine needles, he made his way out of the woods.

The next day, he reached the house of the rich man. However, he was so poor and ragged that the gatekeeper only laughed at him. "How could an old beggar like you help my master?"

The old peddler tried to argue. "Beggar or rich man, we are all one."

But it so happened that the rich man was passing by the gates. He went over to the old peddler. "I said anyone could see me. But it'll mean a stick across your back if you're wasting my time."

The old peddler took out the pouch. "Dissolve this bead in some wine and drink it down." Then, turning the pouch upside down, he shook the tiny bead onto his palm and handed it to the rich man.

The rich man immediately called for a cup of wine. Dropping the bead into the wine, he waited a moment and then drank it down. Instantly the pain vanished. Shortly after that, his eyes healed.

The rich man was so happy and grateful that he doubled the reward. And the kindly old peddler and his family lived comfortably for the rest of their lives.

READING FOR UNDERSTANDING

1. Why is the rich man desperate?

2. Despite having a job as a candy peddler, why is the old man always so poor?

3. What does the peddler do for the ants?

4. What happens in the ruined temple?

5. How does the peddler find the cure?

RESPONDING TO THE STORY

The peddler is respectful and kind to all creatures because he believes that "we are all one." Can you think of another example of how this statement may be true? Explain.

REVIEWING VOCABULARY

Match the correct definition from the column on the right to each word in the column on the left.

1. escort

    a. early, immature forms of an animal

2. tufts

    b. a hard, smooth, shiny varnish

3. omen

    c. bunches of hairs, feathers, grass, etc., growing closely together

4. lacquer

    d. a thing or happening believed to foretell the future

5. larvae

    e. someone or something that accompanies another for protection

THINKING CRITICALLY

1. What do you think the peddler means when he says "we are all one"?

2. Why do you think it's so important to the peddler that he find the cure?

WRITING PROJECTS

1. Write a newspaper article telling the story of how the rich man's eye disease was cured.

2. Write a paragraph explaining the importance of showing kindness to all living creatures.

FLAME
by Willis Lindquist

Have you ever had the urge to free an animal from its cage? Many people feel that animals should be allowed to live in their natural surroundings, and that animals enjoy their freedom just as much as we do.

Mike Hutchinson has just turned fifteen, and he is expecting his father to keep a promise. For years Mike has wanted, more than anything, to catch a beautiful wild stallion that people call Flame. When Mike's plan is put into motion, he learns some things about wild stallions, about himself, and about respect for nature.

VOCABULARY WORDS

spread (spred) a ranch or large piece of land
❖ My uncle's *spread* covers 3,000 acres.

juniper (jo͞o′ni pər) a kind of evergreen shrub
❖ The landscape was dotted with *juniper*.

corral (kə ral′) an enclosure for holding horses or cattle
❖ The cattle were herded into the *corral*.

camouflaged (kam′ə fläzh) disguised to match surroundings
❖ The jeeps are *camouflaged* to look like jungle vegetation.

jumble (jum′bəl) a disorderly heap
❖ The jackrabbit disappeared behind a *jumble* of rocks.

sorrel (sôr′əl) a light reddish-brown horse
❖ The *sorrel* is a beautiful sight as he gallops.

doggedly (dôg′id lē) stubbornly; persistently
❖ The detective *doggedly* tracked down the thief until he caught him.

silhouetted (sil′o͞o et′əd) seen or shown as a dark shape against a light background
❖ In the dark, a tall figure could be seen *silhouetted* against the light of the bonfire.

"**T**omorrow I'll be fifteen," Mike told his father, "and there is only one thing I want: a chance to catch Flame."

For three years Flame, the wild mustang of Blackman's Rock, had been a legend in the cow country. This powerful stallion with fiery mane and tail was as unconquerable as the wild mountain winds he breathed. Many there were who had attempted his capture. All had failed.

Mr. Hutchinson scowled at his son. An attempt to capture Flame would cost a great deal of money, but being the wealthy owner of the Sanora Spread, money was the least of his worries.

"Mike," he said with a sigh. "That's like chasing a shadow. I was hoping you'd grow up and give your attention to the ranch for a change. For two years you've talked of nothing but that horse. It's no good. You could no more own Flame than you could own the stars."

Mike tightened his lips. "Max Denton almost caught him."

"Denton is an expert with wild horses, one of the best in the country," his father reminded him.

"You promised," Mike said grimly, determined not to be talked out of it this time. "You said if I still wanted to have a go at Flame when I turned fifteen, you'd give me the chance."

"Well, it's nonsense," said his father. "But if you insist . . . I suppose you've got a plan."

Mike did have. For weeks he had been studying the habits of Flame and his band of wild horses. He knew the kind of a trap he'd need and exactly where it should be built.

With a dozen ranch hands to help him, he labored for three weeks on the building of a fence across Blackman's valley, a V-shaped fence which he cleverly disguised with juniper and brush. At the bottom of the V was a gate, and beyond it a corral formed by a circular six-feet-high fence of woven wire. When it was completed, even Trimble, the ranch foreman, had to admit it was the most beautiful job of camouflaged fencework he had ever seen.

"Son, you've given a heap of thought to this," he said with admiration. "But that hoss is a smart one. Reckon you can get him to go in?"

Mike nodded confidently. He hadn't been dreaming and planning these last two years for nothing.

"Flame and his band will come in at the head of the valley. Then we'll push them right in. They don't have wings, and there's no place else for them to go. I want twelve riders tomorrow at noon."

The next day was clear and bright, perfect in every way, and he posted the men at the head of the valley behind a jumble of boulders. With Trimble for company, he rode over Blackman's pass into the next valley and concealed himself in a clump of junipers.

"Might have to wait a couple of hours," he explained to Trimble. "Flame always takes his band down this way to water. When he passes that brush, you get out ahead of him and cut him off. I'll swing in behind so they can't turn back. They'll have to take the pass."

Mike studied the valley about him. For him it was an enchanted valley, for it was Flame's private kingdom, his home, which echoed with the sounds of his comings and goings.

Presently they heard a shrill neighing. Mike held his breath, listening to the distant rumble of flying hoofs. Then a magnificent sorrel with four white socks and streaming mane and tail, the color of living flame, swept into sight. With his head held high, he swung down the

slope in an easy ground-eating trot, the sun flashing
on his rippling muscles, his legs driving smoothly
like pistons.

"Jumping jay birds!" gasped Trimble. "What a
beauty!"

Mike's heart hammered. He had watched Flame often,
and always it brought a hurting lump to his throat.

As the big stallion and his band plunged on, he tossed
his head, looking over the countryside as if the whole
world were his. Then suddenly he stopped, head high,
staring at the juniper thicket with suspicion.

"Now!" whispered Mike.

They rode out in different directions. Flame reared
with a snort, wheeling back to his band, trying to lead
them again the way they had come.

"No you don't," said Mike, swinging his horse down
the slope at full gallop.

A moment later the band with Flame in the lead
headed for the pass. Mike gave a shout of triumph.
They were as good as caught. He and Trimble pressed
them hard until they were through the pass. The rest
was up to the boys in the valley.

Mike ran his horse along the ridge to have a clear
view. He saw the boys give chase, saw the band rush
down the valley and into the trap. It was as easy as that.

"We got him!" he shouted to Trimble.

The foreman came galloping up. "Look at Flame go!"
he said. "He's wheeling round and round in that corral
faster and faster. Wait a minute."

Suddenly Flame turned from his circle, cut straight
across the center of the corral and leaped the fence
with a tail-flirting bound. Then he was off, a flaming
streak of speed.

Mike stared speechless until he was lost from sight.

"You'll never get him into a trap like that again,"
Trimble said. "That hoss learns fast."

"I'll get him yet," said Mike.

The next afternoon the men were posted at five-mile intervals through the whole chain of valleys. Trimble found the stallion on a ridge above the corral where he could keep watch on his band, and Trimble gave chase. Several times the big stallion circled back toward the corral, galloping easily. But Trimble hung on doggedly.

After half an hour of furious riding, another rider burst from cover and took up the chase with a fresh horse, and then another, and another, and another. So the afternoon went, and finally, after eight riders had used up their horses with reckless speed, the big stallion swept past the rocks where Mike was hidden.

The stallion was beginning to tire. Foam and sweat and dust streaked his body, and yet he moved in a flowing motion as if scarcely touching the ground. Out over the flat open country he raced, with Mike gaining at every stride.

Mike was chuckling in his throat. It had turned out perfectly. He, Mike Hutchinson, would be the first to drop a rope over the stallion's head. He made his loop, began swinging it.

But Flame was wise in the ways of men. He had heard the whistling of rope before. He stopped suddenly. Then he turned and charged.

Only the freshness of Mike's horse saved them from the murderous attack of slashing hoofs.

Mike almost lost his seat in the saddle, and in the milling confusion that followed, he dropped his loop and it caught in the brush. There was nothing to do but get down and clear it.

With tears in his eyes, he watched the mighty bounds of Flame as he raced on into the open range.

Mike remounted, and as he sat there watching Flame speed into the distance, he noticed that the stallion kept well clear of any place that might serve as a hiding place for another horse and rider. Mike knew then that Flame had learned his lesson well. If they ever attempted the same stunt again, Flame would head at once for open country where they wouldn't have a chance.

He told that to Trimble when he got back to the corral. "It's no use," he said. "We'll never catch him now." A slow smile came to his lips. "But I taught Flame a few more tricks. I think they might save him from others who want to try."

"You could still do it by hiring one of them windmill planes to chase him down," Trimble said, grinning at the tired boy.

"You mean helicopter," said Mike. "That might work all right, if you didn't kill him first. But I couldn't do it. It wouldn't be fair. I—I matched wits with him and I lost, that's all."

Foreman Trimble stroked his chin thoughtfully. "Well, anyway, you caught his band." He looked at the horses milling in the corral. "You got some mighty fine mares in there."

There were some beauties, but at that moment Mike's attention was distracted by a shrill neighing from the ridge above. There, silhouetted against the sunset, standing proudly as if he owned the hills and the sky above him, Flame watched his imprisoned band below.

For a breathless moment, Mike watched. Slowly he went over to the corral gate and opened it wide. There was a thunder of hoofs and a choke of dust as the band streaked out.

"They're yours, Flame," Mike said thickly under his breath. "All yours. And so are the hills."

In his heart, he knew he was glad. These hills would always have their enchantment. And sometime, if he were lucky, he would hear the shrill neighing of Flame somewhere in the distance—Flame, wild and happy and free, in the hills where he belonged.

READING FOR UNDERSTANDING

1. What is the one thing Mike wants for his fifteenth birthday?

2. How does Mike try to catch Flame the first time?

3. What does Mike try after his first attempt fails?

4. What does Mike do with Flame's mares at the end of the story?

5. Why does Mike decide that he won't try to catch Flame again?

RESPONDING TO THE STORY

Mike catches Flame's band of mares but later decides to let them go. Have you or someone you know or have heard or read about ever captured a wild animal and then let it go? Write a paragraph explaining what prompted you or the person to set it free.

REVIEWING VOCABULARY

1. Gerald herded all the cows into the *corral*, or **(a)** shallow pond **(b)** enclosure for holding horses or cattle **(c)** open pasture for grazing.

2. The caterpillar was *camouflaged* in the tree so the bird **(a)** couldn't see it **(b)** ate it **(c)** sang.

3. Something *silhouetted* is **(a)** a dark shape against a light background **(b)** disorderly and unorganized **(c)** not easily caught.

4. The *jumble* of clothes on Melanie's floor made her room look **(a)** clean **(b)** nicely decorated **(c)** messy.

5. A *juniper* is a kind of **(a)** children's toy **(b)** leafy vegetable **(c)** evergreen shrub.

THINKING CRITICALLY

1. Many wild horses are caught and tamed and then used on ranches. Do you think this practice is fair or not? Explain your answer.

2. When Mike's father is trying to persuade Mike to drop his plan of capturing the wild stallion, he tells his son: "You could no more own Flame than you could own the stars." What do you think his father means by this?

WRITING PROJECTS

1. Write a short story about how Mike feels when one day he sees Flame out in the wild again.

2. Write a letter to Mike telling him how you feel about his decision to leave the horses in the wild.

FOUNDERS OF THE CHILDREN'S RAIN FOREST

by Phillip Hoose

Have you ever wanted to help solve a big problem but didn't know where to begin? When you share your ideas with others, you may be surprised to discover how many people have the same desire to help that you do. When you work on it together, the problem may not seem so tough after all.

In rural Sweden a teacher showed her first- and second-grade students pictures of rain forests. She told them how the destruction of rain forests was affecting the entire world. The students decided they had to do something to save the rain forest areas for their own and future generations.

VOCABULARY WORDS

sloths (slôths) slow-moving, tree-dwelling mammals of Central and South America
❖ Two *sloths* hung lazily from the tree branches.

paralyze (par´ə līz) to make unable to move
❖ Some snakebites can *paralyze* a person.

biologist (bī äl´ə jist) a scientist who studies plant and animal life
❖ The *biologist* gave a lecture about life in a jungle.

canopy (kan´ə pē) a roof-like covering
❖ Trees in a rain forest form a *canopy* over the heads of all the plants and animals.

macaw (mə kô´) a large, brightly colored, long-tailed, harsh-voiced parrot of Central and South America
❖ In the courtyard of the restaurant was a *macaw* in a large cage.

ocelots (äs´ə ləts) large wildcats of North and South America that have a yellow or gray coat marked with black spots
❖ The *ocelots* chased the monkeys through the jungle.

It all began in the first week of school when Eha Kern, from the Fagervik School, in the Swedish countryside, showed her forty first- and second-grade students pictures of hot, steamy jungles near the Equator. It was there, she said, that half the types of plants and animals in the whole world could be found. She read to them about monkeys and leopards and sloths, about snakes that can paralyze your nerves with one bite, about strange plants that might hold a cure for cancer, about the great trees that give us oxygen to breathe and help keep the earth from becoming too hot.

And then she told them that the world's rain forests were being destroyed at the rate of one hundred acres a *minute*. In the past thirty years, she said, nearly half the world's rain forests have been cut down, often by poor people who burn the wood for fire. Sometimes forests are cleared to make pastures for cattle that are slaughtered and sold to hamburger chains in the U.S. and Europe. Sometimes the trees are sold and shipped away to make furniture and paper. More often they are just stacked up and burned. At this rate, there might not be any rain forests left in thirty years!

The children were horrified. The creatures of the rain forest could be gone before the students were even old enough to have a chance to see them. It didn't matter that they lived thousands of miles away in cold, snowy Sweden. It seemed to them that their future was being chopped and cleared away.

During the autumn, as the sunlight weakened and the days became short, the Fagervik children continued to think about the rain forest. Whenever they went on walks past the great fir trees on the school grounds, they imagined jaguars crouched in the limbs just above them, their long tails twitching impatiently.

They begged Mrs. Kern to help them think of something—anything—they could do to rescue the creatures of the tropics. And then one afternoon during a music lesson, a student named Roland Tiensuu asked suddenly, "Can't we just *buy* some rain forest?"

The lesson stopped. It was a simple, clear idea that all the others understood at once. The class began to cheer, and then they turned to their teacher. "Please, Mrs. Kern," they said. "Please, won't you find us a forest to buy?"

Mrs. Kern had no idea how to find a rain forest for sale. But then, the very weekend after Roland's idea, she was introduced to an American biologist named Sharon Kinsman. As they chatted, Ms. Kinsman explained that she had been working in a rain forest called Monteverde, or Green Mountain.

When Mrs. Kern told Ms. Kinsman of the nearly impossible mission her students had given her, she expected the biologist to laugh. Instead her expression turned serious. "Oh," she said quickly, "please buy mine."

Ms. Kinsman said that some people in Monteverde were trying desperately to buy land so that more trees wouldn't be cut. Much land had already been protected but much more was needed. Land was cheap there, she said—only about twenty-five dollars per acre.

Ms. Kinsman agreed to visit the Fagervik School. She would bring a map and slides of the Monteverde Forest and tell the children where they could send money to buy rain forest land. When Mrs. Kern told the children what had happened, they didn't even seem surprised. As they put it, "We knew you would find one."

In the days before Sharon Kinsman's visit, the Fagervik students began to think about how to raise money. They asked Mrs. Kern to write down all their ideas. As she picked up a piece of chalk, several children spoke at once.

"Pony rides!"

"Let's collect old things and sell them!"

"What about a rain forest evening here at school?"

"Dog washing!"

Dog washing? They began to laugh. "That would never work," someone said. "Who would give money for that?" Mrs. Kern put her chalk down. "Look," she said. "Let's make this our rule: there are no bad ideas. The only bad thing is if you have an idea and don't say it. Then we can't use it." She returned to the blackboard. Were there more ideas?

"A rabbit jumping contest!"

"Rabbit jumping?" said Mrs. Kern. "Be serious. You can't *make* a rabbit jump."

"Oh, yes, we all have rabbits. We can train them. We can. We *can!*"

Mrs. Kern tried to imagine someone actually paying money to watch children try to make rabbits jump. She couldn't. This idea was crazy.

"Mrs. Kern . . . there's no such thing as a bad idea . . . remember?" She did. "Rabbit jumping," she wrote, dutifully putting her doubts aside.

On November 6, 1987, Sharon Kinsman arrived at the Fagervik School. She was just as enthusiastic as the students. They put on skits for her about rain forests and showed her the many books they had written about tropical creatures. Then at last, it was her turn to show them slides of the Monteverde Forest.

First she unfolded a map of the forest and pointed to the area their money could preserve from cutting. She told them that 400 bird species live in the forest, more than in all of Sweden, as well as 490 kinds of butterflies and 500 types of trees. Monteverde is also the only home in the world, she said, for the golden toad, a creature that seems to glow in the dark.

Then she showed her slides. As the room became dark, the students were swept into a hot, steamy jungle half the world away. The slides took them sloshing along a narrow, muddy trail, crisscrossed with roots and vines. A dark canopy of giant trees, thick with bright flowering plants, closed in above them.

They saw giant spiders and deadly snakes. Ms. Kinsman's tape recorder made the forest ring with the shriek of howler monkeys calling to each other and with the chattering of parrots above the trees. They saw the golden toad, the scarlet macaw, and the red-backed poison-arrow frog.

And they saw the forest disappearing, too. They saw hard-muscled men, their backs glistening with sweat, pushing chain saws deep into the giant trees. They could almost smell the smoke of burning tree limbs and feel the thunder of thick, brown trunks crashing down. Behind great piles of ragged wood, the tropical sky was hazy with smoke. Time seemed very short.

When the lights came on, the students were back in Sweden, but they were not the same. Now they had seen their forest—and the danger it faced. There was no time to lose. Mrs. Kern had inspired them with a problem, and Roland had given them an idea they could work with. Sharon Kinsman had shown them their target. Now it was up to them.

Two weeks later, more than a hundred people crowded into an old school house near the Fagervik School for a rain forest evening. Students stood by the door and collected ten crowns (about $1.50) from each person. Special programs cost another crown.

Even though it was winter, rain splattered steadily onto the roof, just as it must have been raining in the Monteverde Forest. To the students, rain was a good sign.

First they performed a play containing a dramatic scene in which trees of the rain forest were cut and creatures killed. That way guests would understand the problem they were trying to help solve. As the applause died down, the children passed an old hat around, urging audience members to drop money in it.

Then they sold rain forest books and rain forest poems. "We were not afraid to ask for money," remembers Maria Karlsson, who was nine. "We knew what we wanted was important." One boy stood at a table keeping track of how much they were making. Whenever a classmate would hand over a fresh delivery of cash, he would count it quickly and shout above the noise, "Now we've got two hundred crowns!" "Now it's three hundred!!"

The evening's total came to 1,600 crowns, or about $240. The next day, they figured out that they had raised enough money to save about twelve football fields worth of rain forest. It was wonderful . . . but was it enough space for a sloth? A leopard? They all knew the answer. They needed more.

They filled up another blackboard with ideas and tried them out. Everything seemed to work. Mrs. Kern brought in a list of prominent people who might make donations. Two girls wrote a letter to the richest woman on the list. A few days later, a check arrived. Someone else wrote to the king of Sweden and asked if he would watch them perform plays about the rain forest. He said yes.

One day they went to a recording studio and made a tape of their rain forest songs. From the very beginning, Mrs. Kern and a music teacher had been helping them write songs. They started with old melodies they liked, changing them a little as they went along. As soon as anybody came up with a good line, they sang it into a tape recorder so they wouldn't forget it by the end of the song. They rehearsed the songs many times on their school bus before recording them, then designed a cover and used some of their money to buy plastic boxes for the tapes. Within months, they had sold five hundred tapes at ten dollars each.

The more they used their imaginations, the more money they raised. They decided to have a fair. "We had a magician and charged admission," remembers Lis Degeby, who was eight. "We charged to see who could make the ugliest face. We had a pony riding contest. We had a market. We had a lady with a beard. We had the strongest lady in the world. Maria forecast the future in a cabin. We tried everything." The biggest money maker of all was the rabbit jumping contest, even though each rabbit sat still when its time came to jump! Even carrots couldn't budge them. One simply flopped over and went to sleep, crushing its necklace of flowers.

Soon they needed a place to put all the money they had earned. Mrs. Kern's husband, Bernd, helped them form an organization called Barnens Regnskog, which means Children's Rain Forest. They opened a bank account with a post office box where people could continue to mail donations.

By midwinter, they had raised $1,400. The children addressed an envelope to the Monteverde Conservation League, folded a check inside, and sent it on its way to Costa Rica. Weeks later, they received a crumpled package covered with brightly colored stamps. It contained a map of the area that had been bought with their money. A grateful writer thanked them for saving nearly ninety acres of Costa Rican rain forest.

In the early spring, the Fagervik students performed at the Swedish Children's Fair, which led to several national television appearances. Soon schools from all over Sweden were joining Barnens Regnskog and sending money to Monteverde. At one high school near Stockholm, two thousand students did chores all day in the city and raised nearly $15,000. And inspired by the students, the Swedish government gave a grant of $80,000 to Monteverde.

After another year's work, the children of Fagervik had raised $25,000 more. The families who could afford it sent their children to Costa Rica to see Monteverde. Just before Christmas, ten Fagervik children stepped off the plane, blinking in the bright Costa Rican sunlight. It was hot! They stripped off their coats and sweaters, piled into a bus, and headed for the mountains.

A few hours later, the bus turned onto a narrow, rocky road that threaded its way through steep mountains. The children looked out upon spectacular waterfalls that fell hundreds of feet. Occasionally they glimpsed monkeys swinging through the trees.

Ahead, the mountaintops disappeared inside a dark purple cloud. For a few moments they could see five rainbows at once. Soon it began to rain.

The next morning, they joined ten Costa Rican children and went on a hike through the Monteverde Rain Forest. Sometimes the thick mud made them step right out of their boots. But it didn't matter. "There were plants everywhere," says Lia. "I saw monkeys and flowers."

On Christmas day, the children of the Fagervik School proudly presented the staff of the Monteverde Conservation League with their check for $25,000. They said it was a holiday present for all the children of the world.

The Monteverde Conservation League used their gift, and funds that had been donated by other children previously, to establish what is now known as El Bosque Eterno de los Niños, or the Children's Eternal Forest. It is a living monument to the caring and power of young people everywhere. So far, kids from thirty nations have raised more than two million dollars to preserve nearly 33,000 acres of rain forest, plenty of room for jaguars and ocelots. The first group of Fagervik students have now graduated to another school, but the first- and second-graders who have replaced them are still raising great sums of money. The school total is now well over $50,000.

The Fagervik students continue to amaze their teacher. "I never thought they could do so much," Mrs. Kern says. "Sometimes I say to them, 'Why do you work so hard?' They say, 'I think of my future.' They make me feel optimistic. When I am with them, I think maybe anything can be done.'"

READING FOR UNDERSTANDING

1. At what rate does the teacher say the world's rain forests are being destroyed?

2. What are two reasons that people cut down trees in rain forests?

3. How did the teacher find a rainforest to buy?

4. What are three ways that the students raised money?

5. How many acres of rain forest had been saved by children at the time the article was written?

RESPONDING TO THE STORY

Students cared enough about the well-being of the earth to give their time, money, and ideas to save a part of the rain forest from destruction. What can you do to continue their fight to save the rain forest? Discuss your ideas with the class.

REVIEWING VOCABULARY

Fill in each blank with the correct word from the following list: *sloths, paralyze, biologist, macaw, canopy.*

1. Looking up, we caught a glimpse of the brightly colored feathers of a _____ .

2. Shoppers huddled under the _____ at the department store entrance to shelter them from the rain.

3. Severe neck injuries can _____ you.

4. The family of _____ moved slowly from branch to branch.

5. A student interested in plants and animals may want to become a _____ .

THINKING CRITICALLY

1. In what ways is the story of the children's efforts inspirational to you? Write down your answer, and then exchange papers with a partner.

2. List the things the children did when they heard about the destruction of the rain forests. How could these steps be applied to a conservation problem of which you are aware?

WRITING PROJECTS

1. Write a letter to your principal encouraging your school's involvement in a community effort to protect the environment.

2. Write a speech expressing your awareness of some local or global conservation need. Present it to the class.

SEALSKIN, SOULSKIN
by Clarissa Pinkola Estés

How do you feel about your home? Do you feel a special connection to it that you don't feel any other place? When a being is taken from its home, or its true place, it can suffer.

In this tale, an Inuit man has led a life of extreme loneliness. He desperately longs for a companion but has no human friends. One night by moonlight he sees beautiful, unusual women dancing and laughing on top of a large rock in the sea. Among these women, he finds the one who will become his wife. Unfortunately, no matter how much he desires that she belong to him, he cannot change the fact that her true place is somewhere else.

VOCABULARY WORDS

parkas (pär´kəz) hooded fur jackets
❖ Inuits wear *parkas* to protect themselves from the severe cold.

chasms (kaz´əmz) deep cracks
❖ People walking on ice must watch out that they do not fall down into the *chasms*.

kayak (kī´ak´) an Eskimo canoe made of a wood frame covered with skins
❖ The fisherman travels through water by *kayak*.

ice floes (īs flōz) large pieces of floating sea ice
❖ In the arctic sea, the moonlight reflected off the *ice floes* floating by.

outcropping (out´kräp´ing) a place where minerals have emerged from the earth and are visible
❖ The scout hid behind an *outcropping*.

berating (bē rāt´ing) scolding severely
❖ The boy was *berating* his little brother for cheating during the game.

mukluks (muk´luk´) Eskimo boots made of sealskin or reindeer skin
❖ The girl hurriedly put on her *mukluks* before she went outside.

tethered (te*th*´ərd) fastened with a rope or chain
❖ The dog was *tethered* to a tree so she could not run into the street.

During a time that once was, is now gone forever, and will come back again soon, there is day after day of white sky, white snow . . . and all the tiny specks in the distance are people or dogs or bear.

Here, nothing thrives for the asking. The winds blow hard so the people have come to wear their parkas and *mamleks*, boots, sideways on purpose now. Here, words freeze in the open air, and whole sentences must be broken from the speaker's lips and thawed at the fire so people can see what has been said. Here, the people live in the white and abundant hair of old Annuluk, the old grandmother, the old sorceress who is Earth herself. And it was in this land that there lived a man . . . a man so lonely that over the years, tears had carved great chasms into his cheeks.

He tried to smile and be happy. He hunted. He trapped and he slept well. But he wished for human company. Sometimes out in the shallows in his kayak when a seal came near he remembered the old stories about how seals were once human, and the only reminder of that time was their eyes, which were capable of portraying those looks, those wise and wild and loving looks. And sometimes then he felt such a pang of loneliness that tears coursed down the well-used cracks in his face.

One night he hunted past dark but found nothing. As the moon rose in the sky and the ice floes glistened, he came to a great spotted rock in the sea, and it appeared to his keen eye that upon that old rock there was movement of the most graceful kind.

He paddled slow and deep to be closer, and there atop the mighty rock danced a small group of women, naked as the first day they lay upon their mothers' bellies. Well, he was a lonely man, with no human friends but in memory—and he stayed and watched. The women were like beings made of moon milk, and their skin shimmered with little silver dots like those on the salmon in springtime, and the women's feet and hands were long and graceful.

So beautiful were they that the man sat stunned in his boat, the water lapping, taking him closer and closer to the rock. He could hear the magnificent women laughing . . . at least they seemed to laugh, or was it the water laughing at the edge of the rock? The man was confused, for he was so dazzled. But somehow the loneliness that had weighed on his chest like wet hide was lifted away, and almost without thinking, as though he were meant to, he jumped up onto the rock and stole one of the sealskins laying there. He hid behind an outcropping and he pushed the sealskin into his *qutnguq*, parka.

Soon, one of the women called in a voice that was the most beautiful he'd ever heard . . . like the whales calling at dawn . . . or no, maybe it was more like the newborn wolves tumbling down in the spring . . . or but, well no, it was something better than that, but it did not matter because . . . what were the women doing now?

Why, they were putting on their sealskins, and one by one the seal women were slipping into the sea, yelping and crying happily. Except for one. The tallest of them searched high and searched low for her sealskin, but it was nowhere to be found. The man felt emboldened— by what, he did not know. He stepped from the rock, appealing to her, "Woman . . . be . . . my . . . wife. I am . . . a lonely . . . man."

"Oh, I cannot be wife," she said, "for I am of the other, the ones who live *temequanek*, beneath."

"Be . . . my . . . wife," insisted the man. "In seven summers, I will return your sealskin to you, and you may stay or you may go as you wish."

The young seal woman looked long into his face with eyes that but for her true origins seemed human. Reluctantly she said, "I will go with you. After seven summers, it shall be decided."

So in time they had a child, whom they named Ooruk. And the child was lithe and fat. In winter the mother told Ooruk tales of the creatures that lived beneath the sea while the father whittled a bear in whitestone with his long knife. When his mother carried the child Ooruk to bed, she pointed out through the smoke hole to the clouds and all their shapes. Except instead of recounting the shapes of raven and bear and wolf, she recounted the stories of walrus, whale, seal, and salmon . . . for those were the creatures she knew.

But as time went on, her flesh began to dry out. First it flaked, then it cracked. The skin of her eyelids began to peel. The hairs of her head began to drop to the ground. She became *naluaq,* palest white. Her plumpness began to wither. She tried to conceal her limp. Each day her eyes, without her willing it so, became more dull. She began to put out her hand in order to find her way, for her sight was darkening.

And so it went until one night when the child Ooruk was awakened by shouting and sat upright in his sleeping skins. He heard a roar like a bear that was his father berating his mother. He heard a crying like silver rung on stone that was his mother.

"You hid my sealskin seven long years ago, and now the eighth winter comes. I want what I am made of returned to me," cried the seal woman.

"And you, woman, would leave me if I gave it to you," boomed the husband.

"I do not know what I would do. I only know I must have what I belong to."

"And you would leave me wifeless, and the boy motherless. You are bad."

And with that her husband tore the hide flap of the door aside and disappeared into the night.

The boy loved his mother much. He feared losing her and so cried himself to sleep . . . only to be awakened by the wind. A strange wind . . . it seemed to call to him, "Oooruk, Ooorukkkk."

And out of bed he climbed, so hastily that he put his parka on upside down and pulled his *mukluks* only halfway up. Hearing his name called over and over, he dashed out into the starry, starry night.

"Ooooooorukkk."

The child ran out to the cliff overlooking the water, and there, far out in the windy sea, was a huge shaggy silver seal . . . its head was enormous, its whiskers drooped to its chest, its eyes were deep yellow.

"Oooooooorukkk."

The boy scrambled down the cliff and stumbled at the bottom over a stone—no, a bundle—that had rolled out of a cleft in the rock. The boy's hair lashed at his face like a thousand reins of ice.

"Ooooooorukkk."

The boy scratched open the bundle and shook it out— it was his mother's sealskin. Oh, and he could smell her all through it. And as he hugged the sealskin to his face and inhaled her scent, her soul slammed through him like a sudden summer wind.

"Ohhh," he cried with pain and joy, and lifted the skin again to his face and again her soul passed through his. "Ohhh," he cried again, for he was being filled with the unending love of his mother.

And the old silver seal way out . . . sank slowly beneath the water.

The boy climbed the cliff and ran toward home with the sealskin flying behind him, and into the house he fell. His mother swept him and the skin up and closed her eyes in gratitude for the safety of both.

She pulled on her sealskin. "Oh, mother, no!" cried the child.

She scooped up the child, tucked him under her arm, and half ran and half stumbled toward the roaring sea.

"Oh, mother, don't leave me!" Ooruk cried.

And at once you could tell she wanted to stay with her child, she *wanted* to but something called her, something older than she, older than he, older than time.

"Oh, mother, no, no, no," cried the child. She turned to him with a look of dreadful love in her eyes. She took the boy's face in her hands, and breathed her sweet breath into his lungs, once, twice, three times. Then, with him under her arm like a precious bundle, she dove into the sea, down, and down, and down, and still deeper down, and the seal woman and her child breathed easily under water.

And they swam deep and strong till they entered the underwater cove of seals, where all manner of creatures were dining and singing, dancing and speaking, and the great silver seal that had called to Ooruk from the night sea embraced the child and called him grandson.

"How fare you up there, daughter?" asked the great silver seal.

The seal woman looked away and said, "I hurt a human . . . a man who gave his all to have me. But I cannot return to him, for I shall be a prisoner if I do."

"And the boy?" asked the old seal. "My grandchild?" He said it so proudly his voice shook.

"He must go back, father. He cannot stay. His time is not yet to be here with us." And she wept. And together they wept.

And so some days and nights passed, seven to be exact, during which time the luster came back to the seal woman's hair and eyes. She turned a beautiful dark color, her sight was restored, her body regained its plumpness, and she swam uncrippled. Yet it came time to return the boy to land. On that night, the old grandfather seal and the boy's beautiful mother swam with the child between them. Back they went, back up and up and up to the topside world. There they gently placed Ooruk on the stony shore in the moonlight.

His mother assured him, "I am always with you. Only touch what I have touched, my fire sticks, my *ulu*, knife, my stone carvings of otters and seal, and I will breathe into your lungs a wind for the singing of your songs."

The old, silver seal and his daughter kissed the child many times. At last, they tore themselves away and swam out to sea, and with one last look at the boy, they disappeared beneath the waters. And Ooruk, because it was not his time, stayed.

As time went on, he grew to be a mighty drummer and singer and a maker of stories, and it was said this all came to be because as a child he had survived being carried out to sea by the great seal spirits. Now, in the gray mists of morning, sometimes he can still be seen, with his kayak tethered, kneeling upon a certain rock in the sea, seeming to speak to a certain female seal who often comes near the shore. Though many have tried to hunt her, time after time they have failed. She is known as *Tanqigcaq*, the bright one, the holy one, and it is said that though she be a seal, her eyes are capable of portraying those human looks, those wise and wild and loving looks.

READING FOR UNDERSTANDING

1. What is the cause of the man's unhappiness?

2. What does the man want the seal woman to do?

3. Why doesn't the man return the sealskin to his wife after seven years as he promised?

4. Why doesn't Ooruk stay beneath the sea with his mother and grandfather?

5. What becomes of Ooruk when he grows up?

RESPONDING TO THE STORY

The seal woman's natural place is in the sea. That is where she feels she belongs. Some people like to be near the ocean, some in the mountains, some in the desert. Write a paragraph about the natural setting you prefer and how being there makes you feel.

REVIEWING VOCABULARY

Match the correct definition from the column on the right to each word in the column on the left.

1. tethered	**a.** an Eskimo canoe
2. parkas	**b.** deep cracks
3. chasms	**c.** fastened with a rope or chain
4. kayak	**d.** scolding severely
5. berating	**e.** hooded fur jackets

THINKING CRITICALLY

1. When the man took the seal woman's sealskin and asked her to be his wife, she "looked long into his face." What do you think she saw there that made her willing to give up her natural place and be his wife?

2. What do you think the man does not understand about nature?

WRITING PROJECTS

1. The author says: "And Ooruk, because it was not his time, stayed." Write a continuation of the story in which Ooruk goes into the sea to live with his mother and grandfather. Include an explanation of why it is now Ooruk's "time" to live there.

2. Imagine you are Ooruk at the end of the story. Write the lyrics for a song about your special connection to the sea.

FROM *WOODSONG*
by Gary Paulsen

Do you believe that people can learn from animals? Animals can teach us many things when we are willing to observe and learn. Having a respect for all nature helps clear the way to unexpected experiences and insights.

In this excerpt from Woodsong, *Gary Paulsen tells about some of his experiences in Alaska, where he runs trap lines using a dog sled and a team of dogs. One day he watches one sled dog play a funny trick on another sled dog. Paulsen is fascinated by how the dog's mind works, and what he learns from that and other experiences changes his way of life.*

VOCABULARY WORDS

mystified (mis´tə fīd) puzzled

❖ The young child was *mystified* by the strange sight of the ostrich.

alleviate (ə lē´vē āt´) to relieve

❖ My aunt turned on the fans to *alleviate* our discomfort in the hot weather.

contention (kən ten´shən) disputing or quarreling

❖ There was much *contention* among the eight brothers and sisters.

posturing (päs´chər ing) assuming an attitude merely to produce a certain impression

❖ The two roosters were *posturing* before the hens in the barnyard.

compassion (kəm pash´ən) a deep sympathy

❖ The girl felt *compassion* for the abandoned puppies.

exaltation (eg´zôl tā´shən) great joy

❖ The feeling of *exaltation* over finally reaching his home was almost more than the man could bear.

musher (mush´ər) a person who drives a dog sled

❖ Sled dogs respond to the commands of the *musher*.

chagrin (shə grin´) embarrassment or annoyance from having failed or been disappointed

❖ The boy felt overwhelmed by *chagrin* at having fallen off the trampoline.

Cold can be very strange. Not the cold felt running from the house to the bus or the car to the store; not the chill in the air on a fall morning, but deep cold. Serious cold.

Forty, fifty, even sixty below zero—actual temperature, not windchill—seems to change everything. Steel becomes brittle and breaks, shatters; breath taken straight into the throat will freeze the lining and burst blood vessels; eyes exposed too long will freeze; fingers and toes freeze, turn black, and break off. These are all known, normal parts of intense cold.

But it changes beauty as well. Things are steeped in a new clarity, a clear focus. Sound seems to ring and the very air seems to be filled with diamonds when ice crystals form.

On a river in Alaska while training I once saw a place where a whirlpool had frozen into a cone, open at the bottom like a beautiful trap waiting to suck the whole team down. When I stopped to look at it, with the water roaring through at the bottom, the dogs became nervous and stared down into the center as if mystified and were very glad when we moved on.

After a time I stopped trapping. That change—as with many changes—occurred because of the dogs. As mentioned, I had hunted when I was young, trapping and killing many animals. I never thought it wrong until the dogs came. And then it was a simple thing, almost a silly thing, that caused the change.

Columbia had a sense of humor and I saw it.

In the summer the dogs live in the kennel area, each dog with his own house, on a chain that allows him to move in a circle. They can run only with the wheeled carts on cool nights, and sometimes they get bored being tied up. To alleviate the boredom, we give the dogs large beef bones to chew and play with. They get a new bone every other day or so. These bones are the center of much contention—we call them Bone Wars. Sometimes dogs clear across the kennel will hold their bones up in the air, look at each other, raise their hair, and start growling at each other, posturing and bragging about their bones.

But not Columbia.

Usually Columbia just chewed on his bone until the meat was gone. Then he buried it and waited for the next bone. I never saw him fight or get involved in Bone Wars and I always thought him a simple— perhaps a better word would be primitive—dog, basic and very wolf-like, until one day when I was sitting in the kennel.

I had a notebook and I was sitting on the side of Cookie's roof, writing—the dogs are good company for working—when I happened to notice Columbia doing something strange.

He was sitting quietly on the outside edge of his circle, at the maximum length of his chain. With one paw he was pushing his bone—which still had a small bit of meat on it—out and away from him, toward the next circle.

Next to Columbia was a dog named Olaf. While Columbia was relatively passive, Olaf was very aggressive. Olaf always wanted to fight and he spent much time arguing over bones, females, the weather— anything and everything that caught his fancy. He was much scarred from fighting, with notched ears and lines on his muzzle, but he was a very good dog— strong and honest—and we liked him.

Being next to Columbia, Olaf had tried many times to get him to argue or bluster, but Columbia always ignored him.

Until this morning.

Carefully, slowly, Columbia pushed the bone toward Olaf's circle.

And of all the things that Olaf was—tough, strong, honest—he wasn't smart. As they say, some are smarter than others, and some are still not so smart, and then there was Olaf. It wouldn't be fair to call Olaf dumb—dogs don't measure those things like people—but even in the dog world he would not be known as a whip. Kind of a big bully who was also a bit of a doofus.

When he saw Columbia pushing the bone toward him, he began to reach for it. Straining against his chain, turning and trying to get farther and farther, he reached as far as he could with the middle toe on his right front foot, the claw going out as far as possible.

But not quite far enough. Columbia had measured it to the millimeter. He slowly pushed the bone until it was so close that Olaf's claw—with Olaf straining so hard his eyes bulged—just barely touched it.

Columbia sat back and watched Olaf straining and pushing and fighting, and when this had gone on for a long time—many minutes—and Olaf was still straining for all he was worth, Columbia leaned back and laughed.

"Heh, heh, heh . . ."

Then Columbia walked away.

And I could not kill or trap any longer.

It happened almost that fast. I had seen dogs with compassion for each other and their young, and with anger and joy and hate and love but this humor went into me more than the other things.

It was so complicated.

To make the joke up in his mind, the joke with the bone and the bully, and then set out to do it, carefully and quietly, to do it, then laugh and walk away—all of it was so complicated, so complex, that it triggered a chain reaction in my mind.

If Columbia could do that, I thought, if a dog could

do that, then a wolf could do that. If a wolf could do that, then a deer could do that. If a deer could do that, then a beaver, and a squirrel, and a bird, and, and, and . . .

And I quit trapping then.

It was wrong for me to kill.

But I had this problem. I had gone over some kind of line with the dogs, gone back into some primitive state of exaltation that I wanted to study. I wanted to run them and learn from them. But it seemed to be wasteful (the word *immature* also comes to mind) to just run them. I thought I had to have a trap line to justify running the dogs, so I kept the line.

But I did not trap. I ran the country and camped and learned from the dogs and studied where I would have trapped if I were going to trap. I took many imaginary beaver and muskrat but I did no more sets and killed no more animals. I will not kill anymore.

Yet the line existed. Somehow in my mind—and until writing this I have never told another person about this—the line still existed and when I had "trapped" in one area, I would extend the line to "trap" in another, as is proper when you actually trap. Somehow the phony trapping gave me a purpose for running the dogs, and would until I began to train them for the Iditarod, a dogsled race across Alaska, which I had read about in *Alaska* magazine.

But it was on one of these "trapping" runs that I got my third lesson, or awakening.

There was a point where an old logging trail went through a small, sharp-sided gully—a tiny canyon. The trail came down one wall of the gully—a drop of fifty or so feet—then scooted across a frozen stream and up the other side. It might have been a game trail that was slightly widened, or an old foot trail that had not caved in. Whatever it was, I came onto it in the middle of January. The dogs were very excited. New trails always get them tuned up and they were fairly smoking as we came to the edge of the gully.

I did not know it was there and had been letting them run, not riding the sled brake to slow them, and we virtually shot off the edge.

The dogs stayed on the trail but I immediately lost all control and went flying out into space with the sled. As I did, I kicked sideways and caught my knee on a sharp snag, felt the wood enter under the kneecap and tear it loose.

I may have screamed then.

The dogs ran out on the ice of the stream but I fell onto it. As these things often seem to happen, the disaster snowballed.

The trail crossed the stream directly at the top of a small, frozen waterfall with about a twenty-foot drop. Later I saw the beauty of it, the falling lobes of blue ice that had grown as the water froze and refroze, layering on itself. . . .

But at the time I saw nothing. I hit the ice of the stream bed like dropped meat, bounced once, then slithered over the edge of the waterfall and dropped another twenty feet onto the frozen pond below, landing on the torn and separated kneecap.

I have been injured several times running dogs—cracked ribs, a broken left leg, a broken left wrist, various parts frozen or cut or bitten while trying to stop fights—but nothing ever felt like landing on that knee.

I don't think I passed out so much as my brain simply exploded.

Again, I'm relatively certain I must have screamed or grunted, and then I wasn't aware of much for two, perhaps three minutes as I squirmed around trying to regain some part of my mind.

When things settled down to something I could

control, I opened my eyes and saw that my snow pants and the jeans beneath were ripped in a jagged line for about a foot. Blood was welling out of the tear, soaking the cloth and the ice underneath the wound.

Shock and pain came in waves and I had to close my eyes several times. All of this was in minutes that seemed like hours and I realized that I was in serious trouble. Contrary to popular belief, dog teams generally do not stop and wait for a musher who falls off. They keep going, often for many miles.

Lying there on the ice I knew I could not walk. I didn't think I could stand without some kind of crutch, but I knew I couldn't walk. I was a good twenty miles from home, at least eight or nine miles from any kind of farm or dwelling.

It may as well have been ten thousand miles.

There was some self-pity creeping in, and not a little chagrin at being stupid enough to just let them run when I didn't know the country. I was trying to skootch myself up to the bank of the gully to get into a more comfortable position when I heard a sound over my head.

I looked up, and there was Obeah looking over the top of the waterfall, down at me.

I couldn't at first believe it.

He whined a couple of times, moved back and forth as if he might be going to drag the team over the edge, then disappeared from view. I heard some more whining and growling, then a scrabbling sound, and was amazed to see that he had taken the team back up the side of the gully and dragged them past the waterfall to get on the gully wall just over me.

They were in a horrible tangle, but he dragged them along the top until he was well below the waterfall, where he scrambled down the bank with the team almost literally falling on him. They dragged the sled up the frozen stream bed to where I was lying.

On the scramble down the bank, Obeah had taken them through a thick stand of cockleburs. Great clumps of burrs wadded between their ears and down their backs.

He pulled them up to me, concern in his eyes and making a soft whine, and I reached into his ruff and pulled his head down and hugged him and was never so happy to see anybody probably in my life. Then I felt something and looked down to see one of the other dogs—named Duberry—licking the wound in my leg.

She was not licking with the excitement that prey blood would cause but with the gentle licking that she would use when cleaning a pup, a wound lick.

I brushed her head away, fearing infection, but she persisted. After a moment I lay back and let her clean it, still holding on to Obeah's ruff, holding onto a friend.

And later I dragged myself around and untangled them and unloaded part of the sled and crawled in and tied my leg down. We made it home that way, with me sitting in the sled; and later, when my leg was sewed up and healing and I was sitting in my cabin with the leg propped up on pillows by the wood stove; later, when all the pain was gone and I had all the time I needed to think of it . . . later I thought of the dogs.

How they came back to help me, perhaps to save me. I knew that somewhere in the dogs, in their humor and the way they thought, they had great, old knowledge; they had something we had lost.

And the dogs could teach me.

READING FOR UNDERSTANDING

1. How does Gary Paulsen use the dogs and sled at the beginning of the selection?

2. What makes Paulsen change his mind about trapping and killing animals?

3. Why does Paulsen keep the trap line even though he's stopped trapping?

4. How does Paulsen get hurt?

5. What do the dogs do when Paulsen is injured?

RESPONDING TO THE STORY

Gary Paulsen learns something from a dog that gives him a new respect for nature and changes his way of life. Write a short paragraph about someone you know or have heard or read about who has changed his or her life because of something learned from direct contact with nature.

REVIEWING VOCABULARY

1. Damon was so full of *exaltation* when he won the scholarship that he **(a)** became angry **(b)** jumped up and down **(c)** watched television.

2. To *alleviate* her tiredness, Bethany **(a)** went jogging **(b)** tried to stay awake **(c)** took a nap.

3. The unusual turn of events left Martin feeling *mystified*, or **(a)** puzzled **(b)** confident **(c)** worried.

4. There was so much *contention* between the committee members that they **(a)** reached a decision quickly **(b)** couldn't accomplish anything **(c)** brought in more chairs.

5. The *chagrin* I felt after forgetting my line in the play made me want to **(a)** dance **(b)** brag **(c)** hide.

THINKING CRITICALLY

1. If Gary Paulsen was not injured, how would his life be different?

2. Gary Paulsen learns several important things from being around animals. He says that they have something we humans have lost. What do you think he means by this remark?

WRITING PROJECTS

1. What steps can you personally take or can your school or community take to show a greater respect for nature?

2. Write a letter to Gary Paulsen telling him how you feel about his respect for nature and how his story has impacted your life or inspired you.

ZLATEH THE GOAT

by Isaac Bashevis Singer

*Has a parent ever made a decision that was upsetting to
you? Did you ever think that maybe he or she had no
choice? People are sometimes forced to do things because
of need.*

*Reuven's family is very upset by his decision to sell
Zlateh, a goat who has provided milk for them for many
years, to the town butcher. But Reuven has no choice; the
family needs money to buy things to celebrate Hanukkah.
As Aaron, Reuven's twelve-year-old son, is on his way
to town to sell Zlateh, the two are suddenly forced into
a situation in which they must depend on each other
to survive.*

VOCABULARY WORDS

Hanukkah (hä´noo kä) a Jewish holiday that usually falls early in December

❖ Candles are burned for eight nights during *Hanukkah*.

furrier (fʉr´ē ər) a person who processes furs or who makes and repairs fur garments

❖ The *furrier* opened a shop on the town's main street.

eddies (ed´ēz) circular motions of wind or water

❖ The wind blew the snow in *eddies*.

imps (imps) mischievous children

❖ Grandma always called us little *imps* when we got caught sneaking cookies before supper.

cleft (kleft) split

❖ Many animals, such as goats, have *cleft* hooves.

chaos (kā´äs´) extreme disorder

❖ The town was in complete *chaos* after the hurricane.

exuded (eg zōōd´id) spread out in every direction

❖ The bouquet of flowers *exuded* a sweet fragrance.

dreidel (drā´d'l) a game played by spinning a small top; the top used to play the game

❖ During Hanukkah, the children happily played *dreidel* in the evenings.

At **Hanukkah time** the road from the village to the town is usually covered with snow, but this year the winter had been a mild one. Hanukkah had almost come; yet little snow had fallen. The sun shone most of the time. The peasants complained that because of the dry weather there would be a poor harvest of winter grain. New grass sprouted, and the peasants sent their cattle out to pasture.

For Reuven the furrier it was a bad year, and after long hesitation he decided to sell Zlateh the goat. She was old and gave little milk. Feyvel, the town butcher, had offered eight gulden for her. Such a sum would buy Hanukkah candles, potatoes and oil for pancakes, gifts for the children, and other holiday necessaries for the house. Reuven told his oldest boy Aaron to take the goat to town.

Aaron understood what taking the goat to Feyvel meant, but he had to obey his father. Leah, his mother, wiped the tears from her eyes when she heard the news. Aaron's younger sisters, Anna and Miriam, cried loudly. Aaron put on his quilted jacket and a cap with earmuffs, bound a rope around Zlateh's neck, and took along two slices of bread with cheese to eat on the road. Aaron was supposed to deliver the goat by evening, spend the night at the butcher's, and return the next day with the money.

While the family said good-bye to the goat, and Aaron placed the rope around her neck, Zlateh stood as patiently and good-naturedly as ever. She licked Reuven's hand. She shook her small white beard. Zlateh trusted human beings. She knew that they always fed her and never did her any harm.

When Aaron brought her out on the road to town, she seemed somewhat astonished. She'd never been led in that direction before. She looked back at him questioningly, as if to say, "Where are you taking me?" But after a while she seemed to come to the conclusion that a goat shouldn't ask questions. Still, the road was different. They passed new fields, pastures, and huts with thatched roofs. Here and there a dog barked and came running after them, but Aaron chased it away with his stick.

The sun was shining when Aaron left the village. Suddenly the weather changed. A large black cloud with a bluish center appeared in the east and spread itself rapidly over the sky. A cold wind blew in with it. The crows flew low, croaking. At first it looked as if it would rain, but instead it began to hail as in summer. It was early in the day, but it became dark as dusk. After a while the hail turned to snow.

In his twelve years Aaron had seen all kinds of weather, but he had never experienced a snow like this one. It was so dense it shut out the light of the day. In a short time their path was completely covered. The wind became as cold as ice. The road to town was narrow and winding. Aaron no longer knew where he was. He could not see through the snow. The cold soon penetrated his quilted jacket.

At first Zlateh didn't seem to mind the change in weather. She too was twelve years old and knew what winter meant. But when her legs sank deeper and deeper into the snow, she began to turn her head and look at Aaron in wonderment. Her mild eyes seemed to ask, "Why are we out in such a storm?" Aaron hoped that a peasant would come along with his cart, but no one passed by.

The snow grew thicker, falling to the ground in large, whirling flakes. Beneath it Aaron's boots touched the softness of a plowed field. He realized that he was no longer on the road. He had gone astray. He could no longer figure out which was east or west, which way was the village, the town. The wind whistled, howled, whirled the snow about in eddies. It looked as if white imps were playing tag on the fields. A white dust arose above the ground. Zlateh stopped. She could walk no longer. Stubbornly she anchored her cleft hooves in the earth and bleated as if pleading to be taken home. Icicles hung from her white beard, and her horns were glazed with frost.

Aaron did not want to admit the danger, but he knew just the same that if they did not find shelter they would freeze to death. This was no ordinary storm. It was a mighty blizzard. The snowfall had reached his knees. His hands were numb, and he could no longer feel his toes. He choked when he breathed. His nose felt like wood, and he rubbed it with snow. Zlateh's bleating began to sound like crying. Those humans in whom she had so much confidence had dragged her into a trap. Aaron began to pray to God for himself and for the innocent animal.

Suddenly he made out the shape of a hill. He wondered what it could be. Who had piled snow into such a huge heap? He moved toward it, dragging Zlateh after him. When he came near it, he realized that it was a large haystack which the snow had blanketed.

Aaron realized immediately that they were saved. With great effort he dug his way through the snow. He was a village boy and knew what to do. When he reached the hay, he hollowed out a nest for himself and the goat. No matter how cold it may be outside, in the hay it is always warm. And hay was food for Zlateh. The moment she smelled it, she became contented and began to eat. Outside the snow continued to fall. It quickly covered the passageway Aaron had dug. But a boy and an animal need to breathe, and there was hardly any air in their hideout. Aaron bored a kind of a window through the hay and snow and carefully kept the passage clear.

Zlateh, having eaten her fill, sat down on her hind legs and seemed to have regained her confidence in man. Aaron ate his two slices of bread and cheese, but after the difficult journey he was still hungry. He looked at Zlateh and noticed her udders were full. He lay down next to her, placing himself so that when he milked her he could squirt the milk into his mouth. It was rich and sweet. Zlateh was not accustomed to being milked that way, but she did not resist. On the contrary, she seemed eager to reward Aaron for bringing her to a shelter whose very walls, floor, and ceiling were made of food.

Through the window Aaron could catch a glimpse of the chaos outside. The wind carried before it whole drifts of snow. It was completely dark, and he did not know whether night had already come or whether it was the darkness of the storm. Thank God that in the hay it was not cold. The dried hay, grass, and field flowers exuded the warmth of the summer sun. Zlateh ate frequently; she nibbled from above, below, from the left and right. Her body gave forth an animal warmth, and Aaron cuddled up to her. He had always loved Zlateh, but now she was like a sister. He was alone, cut off from his family, and wanted to talk. He began to talk to Zlateh.

"Zlateh, what do you think about what has happened to us?" he asked.

"Maaaa," Zlateh answered.

"If we hadn't found this stack of hay, we would both be frozen stiff by now," Aaron said.

"Maaaa," was the goat's reply.

"If the snow keeps falling like this, we may have to stay here for days," Aaron explained.

"Maaaa," Zlateh bleated.

"What does 'Maaaa' mean?" Aaron asked. "You'd better speak up clearly."

"Maaaa. Maaaa," Zlateh tried.

"Well, let it be 'Maaaa' then," Aaron said patiently. "You can't speak, but I know you understand. I need you and you need me. Isn't that right?"

"Maaaa."

Aaron became sleepy. He made a pillow out of some hay, leaned his head on it, and dozed off. Zlateh too fell asleep.

When Aaron opened his eyes, he didn't know whether it was morning or night. The snow had blocked up his window. He tried to clear it, but when he had bored through to the length of his arm, he still hadn't reached the outside. Luckily he had his stick with him and was able to break through to the open air. It was still dark outside. The snow continued to fall and the wind wailed, first with one voice and then with many. Sometimes it had the sound of devilish laughter. Zlateh too awoke, and when Aaron greeted her, she answered, "Maaaa." Yes, Zlateh's language consisted of only one word, but it meant many things. Now she was saying, "We must accept all that God gives us—heat, cold, hunger, satisfaction, light, and darkness."

Aaron had awakened hungry. He had eaten up his food, but Zlateh had plenty of milk.

For three days Aaron and Zlateh stayed in the haystack. Aaron had always loved Zlateh, but in these three days he loved her more and more. She fed him with her milk and helped him keep warm. She comforted him with her patience. He told her many stories, and she always cocked her ears and listened. When he patted her, she licked his hand and his face. Then she said, "Maaaa," and he knew it meant, I love you too.

The snow fell for three days, though after the first day it was not as thick and the wind quieted down. Sometimes Aaron felt that there could never have been a summer, that the snow had always fallen, ever since he could remember. He, Aaron, never had a father or mother or sisters. He was a snow child, born of the snow, and so was Zlateh. It was so quiet in the hay that his ears rang in the stillness. Aaron and Zlateh slept all night and a good part of the day. As for Aaron's dreams, they were all about warm weather. He dreamed of green fields, trees covered with blossoms, clear brooks, and singing birds. By the third night the snow had stopped, but Aaron did not dare to find his way home in the darkness. The sky became clear and the moon shone, casting silvery nets on the snow. Aaron dug his way out and looked at the world. It was all white, quiet, dreaming dreams of heavenly splendor. The stars were large and close. The moon swam in the sky as in a sea.

On the morning of the fourth day Aaron heard the ringing of sleigh bells. The haystack was not far from the road. The peasant who drove the sleigh pointed out the way to him—not to the town and Feyvel the butcher, but home to the village. Aaron had decided in the haystack that he would never part with Zlateh.

Aaron's family and their neighbors had searched for the boy and the goat but had found no trace of them during the storm. They feared they were lost. Aaron's mother and sisters cried for him; his father remained silent and gloomy. Suddenly one of the neighbors came running to their house with the news that Aaron and Zlateh were coming up the road.

There was great joy in the family. Aaron told them how he had found the stack of hay and how Zlateh had fed him with her milk. Aaron's sisters kissed and hugged Zlateh and gave her a special treat of chopped carrots and potato peels, which Zlateh gobbled up hungrily.

Nobody ever again thought of selling Zlateh, and now that the cold weather had finally set in, the villagers needed the services of Reuven the furrier once more. When Hanukkah came, Aaron's mother was able to fry pancakes every evening, and Zlateh got her portion too. Even though Zlateh had her own pen, she often came to the kitchen, knocking on the door with her horns to indicate that she was ready to visit, and she was always admitted. In the evening Aaron, Miriam, and Anna played dreidel. Zlateh sat near the stove watching the children and the flickering of the Hanukkah candles.

Once in a while Aaron would ask her, "Zlateh, do you remember the three days we spent together?"

And Zlateh would scratch her neck with a horn, shake her white bearded head and come out with the single sound which expressed all her thoughts, and all her love.

READING FOR UNDERSTANDING

1. Why is the family upset about Zlateh being sold?
2. Why does Aaron take Zlateh into the haystack?
3. How do Aaron and Zlateh survive for three days in the haystack?
4. What made Aaron decide he would never part with Zlateh?
5. What happens to Zlateh when they return home?

RESPONDING TO THE STORY

Aaron and Zlateh help each other survive a storm that neither of them could have survived alone. Many people have relationships with animals which are mutually beneficial. For example, some visually impaired people depend on seeing-eye dogs to help them get around safely, and the dogs are fed, sheltered, and cared for in return. Have you or someone you know or have heard or read about had an experience with an animal where both benefited? Write a paragraph describing the situation.

REVIEWING VOCABULARY

Fill in each blank with the correct word from the following list: *exuded, cleft, imps, chaos, eddies.*

1. Karen should have known that having so many children in her house at once would create

   _____ .

2. Circular motions of wind can form _____ .

3. Laurel _____ such happiness that I could tell she was in love.

4. The squealing children were behaving like little _____ in the toy store.

5. Pigs, elk, and deer all have _____ hooves.

THINKING CRITICALLY

1. How does this story show the interdependence between humans and animals? Explain using details from the story.

2. In what ways did Zlateh's position in the household change after the storm?

WRITING PROJECTS

1. Although Zlateh says only one word, Aaron knows she is saying many different things. Write about communicating with a pet you have or have known. Explain how you knew what the pet was saying.

2. Write a short story about yourself and an animal depending on each other. Use your imagination and try to choose an unusual animal for your story rather than something like a dog or a horse.

CUB LIFE
by Joy Adamson

What would you do if you found a baby bird that had been abandoned by its mother? Many of us would want to take on the responsibility of caring for it and seeing to its comfort, or, in other words, show a stewardship of nature. One bird might not be so hard to take care of—but what would you do if you found three baby lions?

In this true story, George Adamson, a game warden in Kenya, kills a lioness in self-defense. He then discovers that she has three newborn cubs hidden in the crack of a rock. The warden takes the cubs to his wife, Joy, who is at a nearby camp. They figure out how to feed the cubs and to take care of their other needs. The house becomes a lion nursery, and the Adamsons learn much from the rapidly growing cubs.

VOCABULARY WORDS

maneuver (mə noo͞o´vər) a movement intended as a skillful step toward an objective
❖ The pilot made a brilliant *maneuver* to land the plane.

fortnight (fôrt´nīt´) two weeks
❖ A *fortnight* had passed before the package finally arrived.

pluckiest (pluk´ ē ist) bravest; most spirited
❖ Despite her small size, the runt of the litter was the *pluckiest* of the three puppies.

reconnoiter (rek´ə noit´ər) to seek out information, to survey
❖ The scout was sent to *reconnoiter* the area.

regurgitate (ri gʉr´jə tāt´) to bring partly digested food back from the stomach to the mouth
❖ A lioness *regurgitates* food to feed her cubs.

quarry (kwôr´ē) anything being hunted or pursued
❖ The mountain lion stalked its *quarry* through the brush.

mandibles (man´də bəl) jaws
❖ Soldier ants have very strong *mandibles* to chew with.

cavalcade (kav´əl kād´) a procession
❖ The *cavalcade* of mules started down the hillside as if on parade.

Early on the morning of the first of February, 1956, I found myself in camp alone with Pati, a rock hyrax who had been living with us as a pet for six and a half years. She looked like a marmot or a guinea pig, though zoologists will have it that on account of the bone structure of its feet and teeth, the hyrax is most nearly related to rhinos and elephants.

Pati snuggled her soft fur against my neck and from this safe position watched all that went on. The country around us was dry with out-crops of granite and only sparse vegetation. All the same, there were animals to be seen; for there were plenty of gerenuk and other gazelles, creatures that have adapted themselves to these dry conditions, and rarely, if ever, drink.

Suddenly I heard the vibrations of a car. This could only mean that George was returning much earlier than expected. Soon our Land Rover broke through the thornbush and stopped near our tents, and I heard George shout, "Joy, where are you? Quick, I have something for you. . . ."

I rushed out with Pati on my shoulder and saw the skin of a lion. But before I could ask about the hunt, George pointed to the back of the car. There were three lion cubs, tiny balls of spotted fur, each trying to hide its face from everything that went on. They were only a few days old, and their eyes were still covered with a bluish film. They could hardly crawl; nevertheless, they tried to creep away. I took them on my lap to comfort them, while George, who was most distressed, told me what had happened. Toward dawn, he and another Game Warden, Ken, had been guided near to the place where the man-eater was said to lie up. When first light broke, they were charged by a lioness who rushed out from behind some rocks. Though they had no wish to kill her, she was very close and the way back was hazardous, so George signalled to Ken to shoot. He hit and wounded her. The lioness disappeared, and when they went forward, they found a heavy trail of blood leading upward. Cautiously, step by step, they went over the crest of the hill till they came to a huge flat rock. George climbed onto it to get a better view, while Ken skirted around below. Then he saw Ken peer under the rock, pause, raise his rifle, and fire both barrels. There was a growl; the lioness appeared and came straight at Ken. George could not shoot, for Ken was in his line of fire. Fortunately, a Game Scout who was in a more favorable position fired his rifle and caused the animal to swerve. Then George was able to kill her. She was a big lioness in the prime of her life, her teats swollen with milk. It was only when he saw this that George realized why she had been so angry and faced them so courageously. Then he blamed himself for not having recognized earlier that her behavior showed that she was defending her litter.

Now he ordered a search to be made for the cubs. Presently he and Ken heard slight sounds coming out of a crack in the rock face. They put their arms down the crevice as far as they could reach. Loud infantile growls and snarls greeted this unsuccessful maneuver. Next they cut a long, hooked stick and after a lot of probing managed to drag the cubs out. They could not have been more than two or three days old. They were carried to the car, where the two biggest growled and spat during the whole of the journey back to camp. The third and smallest, however, offered no resistance and seemed quite unconcerned. Now the three cubs lay in my lap, and how could I resist making a fuss of them?

To my amazement Pati, who was usually very jealous of any rival, soon came to nestle among them, and obviously accepted them as desirable companions.

From that day onward, the four became inseparable. During these early days Pati was the biggest of the company and also, being six years old, was very dignified compared with the clumsy little velvet bags who couldn't walk without losing their balance.

It was two days before the cubs accepted their first milk. Until then, whatever trick I tried to make them swallow diluted, unsweetened, canned milk only resulted in their pulling up their tiny noses and protesting: "ng-ng, ng-ng," very much as we did as children, before we had learned better manners and been taught to say, "No, thank you."

Once they had accepted the milk, they could not get enough of it. Every two hours I had to warm it and clean the flexible rubber tube, which we had taken from the wireless set to serve as a teat until we were able to get a proper baby's bottle. We had sent at once to the nearest African market, which was about fifty miles away, not only for the teat but also for cod-liver oil, glucose, and cases of unsweetened milk. At the same time, we had sent an S.O.S. to the District Commissioner at Isiolo, about a hundred and fifty miles away, announcing the arrival there within a fortnight of Three Royal Babies, asking him to be good enough to have a comfortable wooden home made in time for our return.

Within a few days the cubs had settled down and were everybody's pets. Pati, their most conscientious self-appointed nanny, remained in charge. She was devoted to them, and never minded being pulled and trodden on by the three fast-growing little bullies. All the cubs were females. Even at this age, each had a definite character. The "Big One" had a benevolent superiority and was generous toward the others. The second was a clown, always laughing and spanking her milk bottle with both her front paws as she drank, her eyes closed in bliss. I named her Lustica, which means the "Jolly One."

The third cub was the weakling in size, but the pluckiest in spirit. She pioneered all around, and was always sent by the others to reconnoiter when something looked suspicious to them. I called her Elsa, because she reminded me of someone of that name.

In the natural course of events, Elsa would probably have been the throw-out of the pride. The average number of cubs in a litter is four, of which one usually dies soon after birth, and another is often too weak to be reared. It is for this reason that one usually only sees two cubs with a lioness. Their mother looks after them till they are two years old. For the first year she provides their food. She regurgitates it, thus making it acceptable to them. During the second year, the cubs are allowed to take part in the hunting, but they get severely disciplined if they lose their self-control. Since at this time they are unable to kill on their own, they have to rely for their food on what may be left over from a kill by the full-grown lions of the pride. Often very little remains for them, so they are usually in a bad, scruffy condition at this age. Sometimes they can't bear the hunger. Then either they break through the line of gorging adults and are likely to be killed, or they leave the pride, in small groups; and, because they do not yet know how to kill properly, often run into trouble. Nature's law is harsh and lions have to learn the hard way from the beginning.

The quartet—Pati and the three cubs—spent most of the day in the tent under my camp bed. This evidently seemed to them a safe place and the nearest thing they could find to their natural nursery. They were by nature house-trained and always took great care to reach the sand outside. There were a few accidents during the first days; but afterward, on the rare occasions when a little pool disgraced their home, they meowed and made comical grimaces of disgust. In every way they were wonderfully clean and had no smell except for a very pleasant one like honey—or was it cod-liver oil? Their tongues were already as rough as sandpaper. As they grew older, we could feel them, even through our khaki clothes, when they licked us.

When, after two weeks, we returned to Isiolo, our Royal Babies had a palace awaiting them. Everyone came to see them, and they received a royal welcome. They loved Europeans and especially small children. They took a great liking to a young Somali, called Nuru. He was our garden boy. Now we appointed him guardian and lion-keeper in chief. The post pleased him, for it raised his social status. It also meant that when the cubs got tired of romping all over the house and its surroundings and preferred to sleep under some shady bush, he was able to sit near them for long hours, watching to see that no snakes or baboons molested them.

For twelve weeks we kept them on a diet of unsweetened milk mixed with cod-liver oil, glucose, bonemeal, and a little salt. Soon they showed us that they only required three-hourly feeds, and then gradually the intervals became longer.

By now their eyes were fully opened, but they could not yet judge distances and often missed their target. To help them over this difficulty, we gave them rubber balls and old inner tubes to play with—the latter were perfect for tug-of-war games. Indeed, anything made of rubber, or that was soft and flexible, fascinated them. They would try to take the inner tube from each other, the attacker rolling sideways onto the possessor, pressing her weight between the end of the tube and its owner. If no success was achieved by this method, the rivals would simply pull with all their might. Then, when the battle had been won, the victor would parade with the trophy in front of the others and provoke an attack. If this invitation was ignored, the rubber would be placed in front of their noses, while the owner pretended to be unaware that it might be stolen from her.

Surprise was the most important element in all their games. They stalked each other—and us—from their earliest age, and knew by instinct how to do it properly.

They always attacked from the rear. Keeping under cover, they crouched. They then crept slowly toward the unsuspecting victim until the final rush was made at flying speed, and resulted in the attacker's landing with all her weight on the back of her quarry, throwing it to the ground. When we were the object of such an attack, we always pretended to be unaware of what was going on. Obligingly we crouched down and looked the other way until the final onslaught took place. This delighted the cubs.

Pati always wanted to be in the game; though, as the cubs were soon three times her size, she took good care to keep out of the way of heavy spankings and to avoid being squashed by her charges. In all other circumstances, she retained her authority by sheer character. If the cubs became too aggressive, she put them in their places by just turning around and facing them. I admired her spirit, for, small as she was, it needed a lot of courage to convince them of her fearlessness; the more so that her only defenses were her sharp teeth, quick reactions, intelligence, and pluck.

When the cubs were three months old, they had teeth big enough to make it possible for them to eat meat. So now I gave them raw minced meat, which was the best we could do to imitate their mother's regurgitated food. For several days they refused to touch it and pulled grimaces of disgust. Then Lustica made the experiment and found it to her taste. The others took courage from her, and soon there was a fight at every meal. This meant that poor Elsa, who was still weaker than the others, had little chance of getting her fair share; so I kept the tidbits for her and used to take her on my lap for meals. She loved this. Rolling her head from side to side and closing her eyes, she showed me how happy she was. At these times, she would suck my thumbs and massage my thighs with her front paws as though she were kneading her mother's belly in order to get more milk. It was during these hours that the bond between us developed. We combined playing with feeding, and my days were happily spent with these charming creatures.

They were lazy by nature, and it needed a lot of persuasion to get them to move from a comfortable position. Even the most desirable marrow bone was not worth the effort of getting up, and they would roll into position to get at it by the easiest way. But best of all, they liked me to hold their bone for them while they lay on their backs, paws in the air, and sucked at it.

When the cubs went into the bush, they often had adventures. One morning I was following them, for I had given them a worming powder and wished to see the result. I saw them a little way off, asleep. Suddenly I noticed a stream of black soldier ants approaching them. Indeed, some were already climbing up their bodies. Knowing how fiercely these ants will attack anything that lies in their path and how powerful their mandibles are, I was just about to wake up the cubs when the ants changed their direction.

Soon afterwards, five donkeys approached and the cubs woke up. This was the first time they had seen such big animals, and they certainly showed the proverbial courage of a lion, for they all charged simultaneously. This put them into such good heart that when, a few days later, our forty pack donkeys and mules came near the house, the three little lions fearlessly put the whole cavalcade to flight.

At five months they were in splendid condition and getting stronger every day. They were quite free except at night, when they slept in an enclosure of rock and sand which led off from their wooden shelter. This was a necessary precaution, for wild lions, hyenas, jackals, and elephants frequently roam around our house. Any of these might have killed them.

The more we grew to know the cubs, the more we loved them, so it was hard to accept the fact that we could not keep forever three fast-growing lions. Regretfully we decided that two must go and that it would be better that the two big ones, who were always together and less dependent on us than Elsa, should be the ones to leave. Our African servants agreed with our choice; when asked their opinion, they unanimously chose the smallest. Perhaps they were influenced by visions of the future and thought: "If there must be a lion in the household, then let it be as small as possible."

As to Elsa, we felt that if she had only ourselves as friends she would be easy to train, not only for life at Isiolo but also as a travelling companion on our safaris.

As a home for Lustica and the Big One, we chose the Rotterdam-Blydorp Zoo and made arrangements for them to make the journey by air.

Since they would have to leave from the Nairobi airfield, which was one hundred and eighty miles away, we decided to get them accustomed to motoring, and took them for short daily trips in my one-and-a-half-ton truck, which had a wired box body. We also began to feed them in it, so that they might get used to it and consider it as one of their play pens.

On the last day, we padded the car with soft sandbags.

When we drove off, Elsa ran a short way down the drive; and then she stood with the most mournful expression in her eyes, watching the car in which her two sisters were disappearing. I traveled in the back with the cubs and had armed myself with a small first-aid kit, fully expecting to be scratched during the long journey. However, my medical precautions were put to shame; for, after an hour of restlessness, the cubs lay on the bags beside me, embracing me with their paws. We traveled like this for eleven hours, delayed by two blowouts. The lions could not have been more trusting. When we reached Nairobi, they looked at me with their large eyes, puzzled to know what to make of all the strange noises and smells. Then the plane carried them off forever from their native land.

After a few days, we received a cable announcing the safe arrival of our cubs in Holland. When I visited them, about three years later, they accepted me as a friendly person and allowed me to stroke them, but they did not recognize me. They live in splendid conditions and, on the whole, I was glad to know that almost certainly they had no recollection of a freer life.

READING FOR UNDERSTANDING

1. How does the lioness react to the wardens?

2. How do the Adamsons feel about the cubs?

3. Who is Pati and what is her role in the cubs' life?

4. How do the cubs show their natural instincts when they play?

5. Why do the Adamsons choose Elsa to keep?

RESPONDING TO THE STORY

The Adamsons soon find that three growing lions are too much for one household. How do you feel about people taking wild animals into their homes? Write a paragraph explaining why you feel as you do.

REVIEWING VOCABULARY

Match the correct definition from the column on the right to each word in the column on the left.

1. reconnoiter   **a.** jaws

2. cavalcade   **b.** to seek out information

3. regurgitate   **c.** procession

4. maneuver   **d.** to bring partly digested food back from the stomach to the mouth

5. mandibles   **e.** a movement intended as a skillful step toward an objective

THINKING CRITICALLY

1. Do you think the Adamsons did the right or wrong thing in saving the cubs, only to have them later live outside their natural habitat in a zoo? Give reasons for your answer.

2. Why do you think the Adamsons did not return the growing lions to the game preserve where they were found? Discuss several possible reasons.

WRITING PROJECTS

1. Write one or two paragraphs about what you see as the positive and negative aspects of zoos. How do you think zoos fit in with people's stewardship of nature?

2. Write a short story describing what you think would happen if you brought three lion cubs into your household. Who would care for them and how?

ACKNOWLEDGMENTS

For "The Wise Master," "The Wooden Sword," and "How War Was Ended": From *Wisdom Tales from Around the World* by Heather Forest **(August House, 1996)**. Copyright 1996 by Heather Forest. Reprinted by permission of the publisher. For "Sealskin, Soulskin": From WOMEN WHO RUN WITH THE WOLVES by Clarissa Pinkola Estés, Ph.D. Copyright © 1991 by Clarissa Pinkola Estés, Ph.D. All rights including but not limited to performance, derivative, adaptation, musical, audio and recording, illustrative, theatrical, film, pictorial, reprint and electronic are reserved. Used by kind permission of the author, Dr. Estés. Reprinted by permission of **Ballantine Books, a division of Random House, Inc**. For "The Dancing Kettle" and "The Old Man of the Flowers": From *The Dancing Kettle and Other Japanese Folk Tales* by Yoshiko Uchida. Permission granted by **Creative Arts Book Company**, Berkeley, California. For "The Parable of the Eagle": From *Mosaics: Folktales from Around the World* by Melissa Billings. Reprinted by permission of **CURRICULUM ASSOCIATES®, Inc**. For "Diary of a Young Girl": From THE DIARY OF A YOUNG GIRL THE DEFINITIVE EDITION by Anne Frank, Otto H. Frank & Mirjam Pressler, Editors, & translated by Susan Massotty. Translation copyright © 1995 by Doubleday, a division of Bantam Doubleday Dell Publishing Group, Inc. Used by permission of **Doubleday, a division of Bantam Doubleday Dell Publishing Group, Inc**. Also for "The Richer, The Poorer": From THE RICHER, THE POORER by Dorothy West. Copyright © 1995 by Dorothy West. Used by permission of **Doubleday, a division of Bantam Doubleday Dell Publishing Group, Inc**. For "Navajo Code Talker": From RIO GRANDE STORIES, copyright © 1994 by Carolyn Meyer. Reprinted by permission of **Harcourt Brace & Company**. Also for "The No-Guitar Blues": From BASEBALL IN APRIL AND OTHER STORIES, copyright © 1990 by Gary Soto. Reprinted by permission of the **Harcourt Brace & Company**. For "We are All One": From from THE RAINBOW PEOPLE by Laurence Yep. Text copyright © 1989 by Laurence Yep. Used by permission of **HarperCollins Publishers**. Also for "Zlateh the Goat": From ZLATEH THE GOAT AND OTHER STORIES by Isaac Bashevis Singer. Text copyright © 1966 by Isaac Bashevis Singer. Used by permission of **HarperCollins Publishers**. For